FATE'S
BOOKIE

FATE'S BOOKIE
HOW THE LOTTERY SHAPED THE WORLD

GARY HICKS

Illustrations by Simon Groves

First published 2009

The History Press
The Mill, Brimscombe Port
Stroud, Gloucestershire, GL5 2QG
www.thehistorypress.co.uk

British Library Cataloguing in Publication Data.
A catalogue record for this book is available from the British Library.

ISBN 978 0 7509 4972 9

Typesetting and origination by The History Press
Printed in Great Britain

CONTENTS

WHAT THEY SAID

For

Allotment determines offices, power is held accountable and deliberation is conducted in public   Herodotus

Indispensable to the existence of man   Thomas Jefferson

This most generous diffuser of universal happiness   Charles Lamb

The suffrage by lot is natural to democracy   Montesquieu

It was their delight, their folly, their anodyne, their intellectual stimulant   George Orwell

Against

The folly of appointing public officials by lot   Xenophon

No appointment by lot … can be generally good in a government conversant in extensive subjects   Edmund Burke

It annually sends unhappy victims to the Hulks, Botany Bay, and the Gallows   *The Gentleman's Magazine*, 1816

There would never be a fair Lottery   Adam Smith

I do not think that the Government should encourage more gambling   Margaret Thatcher

PREFACE

London, Thursday 18 October 1826

For hours, at Coopers' Hall in the City of London, traditional venue of lottery draws, huge crowds had filled the gallery to overflowing. Outside, so many excited people had gathered in Basinghall Street to witness an historic event that it was virtually impassable. Lottery offices across the capital were besieged by players waiting to hear their fortune. For this was no ordinary draw. After 132 years, Parliament had finally voted to put an end to the state lottery, which had become irrevocably mired in fraud and corruption. It was permitted one last fling, marketed amid unprecedented publicity, as 'positively the last lottery that will ever be held in England.' As usual, doctors stood by to treat any players whose blood pressure soared dangerously on hearing their luck, or lack of it. As usual, pickpockets worked the distracted crowd whose attention was fixed on two huge drums, six feet high, rotating faster and faster, each containing tens of thousands of tickets. At a signal from the presiding officer, they were stopped and a Bluecoat boy from Christ's Hospital drew a ticket number from one, while another boy drew its fate, either a prize or a blank, from the other. For ninety minutes this elaborate ritual, which had varied little over the centuries, was repeated until all the tickets were pulled out.

Only one person present won a major prize; a little man who buttoned up his coat and coolly walked off without saying a word. The expectant smiles of everyone else quickly turned to grim-faced dissatisfaction. There was deep suspicion of a fix; the contractors, it was alleged, had kept back many tickets for themselves so that they could win at least half the prizes. That night there were fifty suicides among unsuccessful players, according to an unsubstantiated claim by United States evangelists.

'Yesterday afternoon, at about half past six o'clock,' recorded *The Times* of 19 October 1826, 'that old servant of the state, the Lottery, breathed its last, having for a long period of years, ever since the days of Queen Anne, contributed largely towards the public revenue of the country.'

Triumphant abolitionists, led by anti-slave trade icon William Wilberforce, had campaigned twenty years for this day and were overjoyed that Britain was rid of the 'scourge' of lotteries forever. It was never going to be that easy.

Lotteries are as old as time. The ancient Egyptians, Assyrians and Norsemen all used dice for the casting of lots. The Picts of Scotland put pieces of dough in a pot, some white and some blackened. According to the Old Testament, Moses distributed land west of the River Jordan by lot (as Oliver Cromwell did with the land he conquered in Ireland). In the New Testament, one of the apostles, Matthias, was chosen by lot to fill the place of Judas Iscariot. And Roman soldiers cast lots for Christ's garments at the Crucifixion.

For 1,000 years, at the Delphic oracle in northern Greece, a primitive lottery of coloured broad beans drawn by a priestess decided the fate of kings and empires. Much more sophisticated lotteries were used by the Greeks to elect all their politicians and civil servants, and by the Romans to rebuild Rome after the Civil War. The invention of the zero made possible the drawing of lots on a grand scale – an essential prerequisite of the modern game.

Today, two in three adults play regularly in the UK National Lottery, which has raised more than £22 billion for good causes, from £2.2 billion for the 2012 Olympic Games to a £6,000 grant which saved temporarily Wales's smallest cinema, a converted railway carriage near Swansea. Today, the world lottery market amounts to more than US $200 billion in annual sales; some 140 state lotteries flourish in seventy-five countries; and the prospect of a global lottery with a £500 million top prize is no longer a fantasy. Wilberforce and his disciples must be spinning in their graves.

Moralists have always condemned the lottery as encouraging the belief that success has more to do with luck and chance than hard work or moral values. True, it has long been associated with fraud, corruption and greed, yet it has also delivered huge benefits by raising funds for projects from the Great Wall of China onwards.

In the UK it built the British Museum and Westminster Bridge, provided London with its first clean drinking water, helped pay ransoms to redeem British slaves on the north African Barbary coast, and saved the colony of Virginia, Britain's first permanent settlement in North America, from extinction.

In the United States, using the game for the public good dates back to the earliest colonial times when it was a substitute for taxation. Following the Revolution, it funded worthy schemes, including Harvard and Yale universities. Today, 210 million Americans play the lottery which provides more than 250,000 jobs in thirty-eight states. Since its resurrection in 1964, a staggering total of $200 billion has been raised for government spending. In New York, California, Oregon and New Hampshire, it buys better education for children. In Pennsylvania it buys health care for the elderly. In Arizona it helps pay for transport systems. It funds prisons in Kansas and public sector pensions in Indiana.

Elsewhere, the Tattersall's lottery in Australia built Sydney Opera House and now provides hospitals and medical equipment. In Europe, the first state to seek profit from lotteries was France in 1539; now they are national institutions raising funds for good causes ranging from cancer research to sports stadiums. Spain's much loved El Gordo – the fat one – is the world's biggest and most generous lottery. Played by nine out of ten Spaniards (they got a record £1.4 billion payout in the 2006 Christmas draw), it helped stage the 1992 Olympic Games in Barcelona. The Netherlands has the oldest continuously running draw, dating back to 1726. For centuries, lotteries have also provided relief during times of natural disasters. The wholesale breaching of sea dykes in seventeenth-century Holland, the horrific hurricane of monster hailstones that devastated whole swathes of rural France in 1788 and the catastrophic flooding of southern Louisiana in 1890, are prime examples.

Today, the game is marketed as fun, a little flutter that cheers people up and cannot be compared to an addiction to roulette or blackjack. People were just as irrational and superstitious in the way they selected numbers centuries ago as they are now. *The Spectator* magazine for 9 October 1711 disclosed that some players in that year's lottery chose 1711 as being 'the year of our Lord', others 666 as the Number of the Beast since 'evil men are the most fortunate', 12,000 because it was the number of pounds in the top prize, while others chose birthdays, or numbers seen in dreams or visions .On 11 September 2002, the first anniversary of the terrorist attacks on New York's World Trade Center, balls in the city's draw spookily came out as 9, 11. Yet nearly 6,000 players had selected those numbers.

Lottery fans argue that everyone wins. A ticket, they say, is only a pound, but that amount buys a big dream. More than 250 years ago the diarist Charles Lamb made the same point most eloquently in a celebrated essay. That is not all the ticket buys, runs the argument; there are many benefits, from winners and good causes to the thousands employed in running the game. What is happening now only reflects, though on a much wider and sophisticated scale, the kind of social and economic benefits that the lottery has always provided. It is a willing tax since no-one is compelled to pay and is not as regressive a tax (hitting the poor harder than the rich) as it might appear. And the modern-day lottery is much fairer since its elaborate technological systems practically eliminate the possibility of fraud.

Critics retort that ticket sales can fluctuate wildly and are no substitute for stable, long-term funding for social aims. Complaints are also growing that money is being diverted to causes that were once funded by taxation, in a betrayal of the original vision of promoting access to sport and to the arts for the less wealthy. The row over lottery money 'stolen' for the 2012 Olympics rumbles on. However, provided revenue-raising is professionally managed and tightly regulated, lotteries are invaluable to help pay for public services and amenities that otherwise people might do without.

Governments of all ideologies have used them, from the capitalist United States to communist Russia, where they took off during the Stalinist 1930s. Yet the attitude of our rulers has always been ambivalent, welcoming the revenues raised as a supplement to taxation but decrying any social ills caused. That is why lotteries are forbidden from time to time. Britain's state lottery, which made its debut in 1694, and from 1776 became a regular institution authorised annually by Parliament, was banned in 1826 and did not reappear for 168 years. During the nineteenth century, most lotteries were discontinued elsewhere in Europe (with the exception of Denmark, Spain, Portugal, Austria, the Netherlands) and, eventually, in the United States.

The end of the Second World War led to the re-emergence of national and state lotteries worldwide, a process that accelerated during the 1980s as Governments, reverting to an older tradition, woke up to the possibilities of the game as a nice little earner.

If history teaches us anything, it is that lotteries go in political and economic cycles. On the precedent of the last two great lottery booms of 1693–1720 and 1795–1826, both linked to the gambling fever then gripping the nation, the UK National Lottery probably has about ten years to run before people get tired of it.

However, support appears to be growing for using random selection as a method to further public policy and political aims. Jurors have always been chosen at random. During the Second World War, more than 47,000 young British men, the Bevin Boys, were also selected this way to mine coal as part of the war effort. The United States sent men to both world wars, Korea and Vietnam by lottery and has an elaborate lottery in reserve in the event of a military draft being introduced for Iraq and Afghanistan. Every year another 50,000 immigrants enter the US as a result of the lucky draw. Lotteries are already being used to elect citizens' assemblies, while in the UK support is growing for randomly appointing some peers to newly reformed House of Lords. Councils nationwide are also considering following Brighton and Hove's controversial lead in allocating places to its most popular, over-subscribed schools by lottery. One of the big ideas of Gordon Brown's premiership is citizens' jury service whereby ordinary voters are randomly selected to advise on public policy issues.

So, while economic lotteries may be heading for a downward curve over the next decade, political lotteries, for the first time in many centuries, seem to be on a roll. Not since the year 1659, on the cusp between the death of Olivier Cromwell and the restoration of the monarchy, has government-by-lottery been seriously proposed in the UK. But now, the vision of those early radicals is beginning to glimmer faintly in Brown's Britain, tentatively encouraged by a Prime Minister presented as an intellectual with an appetite for ideas and bent on constitutional change.

Whatever direction it takes, the lottery – with its scandals and benefits, saints and sinners and deep ambivalence of governments – will always be with us. There is no mystery why this is so. The game appeals deeply to the human spirit. Fate alone controls the draw, creating winners and losers in a genuinely democratic way, its very impartiality reflecting the randomness of all life. Fate's bookie indeed.

"OH NO, I'VE DRAWN 'MINISTER FOR
FUNDING THE NEXT OLYMPICS!'"

I

GREEK GODS

Homer's *Iliad* records how Greek heroes each marked their own
lots and put them into Agamemnon's helmet in order to decide
who would fight the Trojan warrior Hector.

This may have been an inspiration. From about 500–321 BC
virtually all political and public post-holders in Athens were
selected by lottery. This complex system, designed to combat fraud,
corruption, cronyism, and prejudiced party politics, was regarded
as supremely democratic since it shared so widely (women and
slaves excepted) the experience and responsibility of office.

Precise comparisons with today are difficult. But imagine half
of those entitled to vote in UK elections serving as a Member of
Parliament for at least a year at some time in their lives. Imagine, too,
Cabinet ministers being appointed by lottery, taking turns to be prime
minister, and directing senior civil servants, themselves appointed by
lottery for one year only, with re-appointment forbidden.

How did the Greeks come by such a unique and innovative democracy-by-lottery which ran Athens so much more efficiently than other ancient cities, and indeed many modern states? The answer lies in religion. A lottery, along with omens and dreams, was one of many rituals whereby the Greek gods advised on the appointment of priests. Divine guidance was sought through simply placing white and black beans in an urn or basket and drawing them out to answer a list of questions. A black bean meant 'No'; a white bean meant 'Yes.'

Gradually, this primitive procedure to allow a god to choose his representative on earth became secularised; as early as 683 BC the lot was used for the annual selection of the Archons, nine officials created to take over the powers of the king. They owed their seats 'to the bean', as the historian Thucydides put it.

The method was rough and ready. If, say, there were nine candidates for six places, six white beans were put in the urn along with three black beans. Sometimes the beans were drawn by the candidates themselves, an unsatisfactory procedure as sleight of hand could easily substitute one drawn bean for another concealed in the palm of the hand. Sometimes the draw was done by state officials who were themselves selected by lottery and rotated regularly to prevent the frequent attempts at bribery. 'For if the same man were repeatedly employed in this duty, he might tamper with the results', warned the philosopher Aristotle. From the start, lotteries were to attract fraudsters as jam attracts wasps.

Democracy-by-lottery reached its zenith in the 180-year period up to 321 BC when the constitution was overthrown by next-door Macedon. All free male citizens took part in this communal decision-making experiment (rivalled today only by the Swiss system of referenda). The total franchise never exceeded 30,000 at its highest, but its limitations should be seen in the context of the time; only in 1969 was everyone over the age of eighteen given the right to vote in United Kingdom elections. More important were the underlying principles as the Greeks saw them: elected assemblies can be essentially undemocratic since they give power to those who want it; lottery-selected civil servants are more receptive than those appointed bureaucratically; party politics as opposed to random rotation of office encourages nepotism and corruption. Theseus, mythical founder of Athens, eloquently makes these points in Euripides' play *The Suppliant Women*. Defending the city against the criticism of a foreigner, he argues that the lottery ensures equal political power and thus secures life and property.

Under the Athenian system, there was an assembly, the sovereign body of the state open to all adult male citizens; this determined policy. The council of Five Hundred, appointed annually by lottery from the ten tribes of Athens, carried it out. All male citizens were eligible to serve on the council as soon as they reached the age of thirty. A fifty-strong committee called the Prytany, loosely equivalent to modern Cabinets, presided over council meetings and looked after such matters as the price of corn, poets' pay and restoring the triremes (warships with three banks of oars). Members of each tribe formed, in turn, the Prytany for thirty-five days each in the lunar year. The Prytany Chairman, appointed by lottery, took office for twenty-four hours only and was not allowed to serve longer or to serve a second term.

With the exception of ambassadors and top military commanders, and some specialist posts such as architects, the normal system of selection to the body of 1,400 public officials who administered Athens was by lottery. This was designed to prevent fraud and collusion in cooking the books. In each department of state the top ten civil servants, chosen one from each tribe, was appointed annually in this way. After a year supervising work done by slaves or outsourced to contractors, they were stood down and could never again be appointed.

This is not as silly as it may sound. Take the inspectors of dockyards, who ran a prototype defence procurement agency. If the appointments had lasted for a number of years, the inspectors might have been tempted to take backhanders from the trireme builders and contractors such as timber merchants supplying wood for oars, whose work they were supposed to be inspecting. And, had they been elected, the rich ship-owners would have tried to rig the vote to get an inspector in their pocket, as has happened countless times since with defence contracts. The fact that the inspectors were drawn at random from across the social spectrum – even the high-born philosopher Plato once served for a year – ensured both diverse experience and a guarantee against fraud.

Work varied widely. City magistrates looked after health and safety, ensuring that rubbish was not dumped within a mile of the city wall and that overhead drainpipes did not pour onto the street. There were temple repairers, auditors, accountants, statisticians, examiners and market magistrates to see that grapes were fresh and weights untampered with, as well as corn guardians and road builders who supervised public slaves.

Even executioners were appointed by lottery. These doubled as jailers, with the right to impose the death penalty, which they carried out themselves (usually by garrotting). So too were 1,600 archers, 1,200 cavalrymen, 500 guards of the dockyards, 50 guards of the Acropolis, and the 6,000 men required for public law suits needing 500-, 1,000- or 1,500-strong panels of jurors. All cases had to be completed within a day, another possible lesson for us.

By necessity, lottery techniques were much more complex and sophisticated than the slapdash beans-in-an-urn method. Dice were used first, then wooden or stone counters, and finally white and black cubes made of bronze which popped out of ingeniously constructed stone, supplanting earlier wooden, allotment machines. These miracles of early mechanics, which the Greeks called *kleroterions*, were first mentioned as long ago as 390 BC by the Greek comedy writer and satirist, Aristophanes. They worked remarkably like the machines that shoot out the winning numbers at the climax of the Camelot draw on national television.

Each machine, which varied from shoebox to gravestone in size, had a tube on an open funnel on the top and a release mechanism at the bottom. Inside, arranged symmetrically in vertical and horizontal rows, were columns of slots which ranged in number from just twelve to as many as 550. Like Camelot's lottery balls the cubes, once released, slid into some kind of display gallery, thus deliberately exposing the draw in full public view.

Selection was rigorously fair and scrupulous, with many checks and balances. Tickets (of bronze plaques) assigned to those taking part were dropped into the columns, black and white cubes shook into the machine's funnel and were then released against each ticket in procedures which varied in complexity from using one white cube among nine black cubes on nine different occasions (to choose ten men) to simply using cubes inscribed with the ticket names or numbers. Even so, attempts were made to fiddle the draw. Demosthenes, statesman and scholar, complained about the practice of 'having the name of the same man entered on two tickets.'

Another method was to use fired clay lottery tokens of rectangular shape which were cut into two and then reassembled jigsaw fashion in an early game of Pelmanism; the prize for reuniting two pieces into a complete token was a job as a minor magistrate.

Aristotle liked lotteries. In a meticulous description in his *The Athenian Constitution* on selecting jurors, he throws splendid light on how the machines worked:

> The archon, when he has inserted the cubes, draws lots on the machine for the tribe. There are bronze cubes, some black and some white: according to the number of jurors to be picked, white cubes are inserted to such a number that there shall be one cube for five tickets; and the black are added on the same principle ...

It is possible the allotment machines were refined for use in the prize lotteries which livened up the spectacular banquets laid on by both the Greeks and Romans. In 1904, a strange calcium-encrusted bronze mechanism, presumed to be made in Greece, was discovered by sponge divers in the wreckage of a Roman cargo ship that sank off the small island of Antikythera in 80 BC. Known as the Antikythera mechanism, the device was originally mounted on a wooden frame and measured 13 inches high,

6.75 inches wide and 3.5 inches thick. There were dials on the outside and a complex assembly of thirty separate differential bronze gears and wheels within. The teeth, arranged very regularly, were formed through equilateral triangles and fitted closely with the wheels, like the inside of a modern wind-up alarm clock. Greek inscriptions totalling 2,000 characters along with astrological signs decorated the mystery object, surely one of the world's oldest mechanical devices.

Technology historians debate its use. Some say it is the first analogue computer, employed to track the motions of the sun, moon and the five planets then known for astrologically auspicious occasions such as religious events or births. Other specialists, including astrophysicists, speculate it is a navigational instrument of some kind. However, in the first century BC, the Roman politician Cicero described a similar instrument as being for 'after-dinner entertainment.' Herein lies the clue that the gadget might also easily have been a luxury toy: a primitive fruit machine. Its mechanism would have been ideal for selecting, by clicking up a combination of astrological signs and letters on its dials, winning tickets in the prize draws held to spice up the banquets. More fun for the emperor than dipping into a guard's helmet for tickets

For more than 1,000 years the lot was also used extensively in oracles throughout Greece to relay the views of the gods. These early versions of the TV quiz show, eventually banned in AD 391, were very popular; distinguished 'customers' allegedly included Alexander the Great, Helen of Troy, the philosopher Aristotle and the mathematician Pythagoras. (Dreaming was also used as a medium; a technique remarkably like today's Italian lotteries, where the newspaper columnist 'Scorpio' regularly foresees lottery results in a dream.) Not all enquirers were happy with the famously ambiguous replies, certainly not the Lydian ruler, King Croesus. The oracle predicted that if he attacked the Persians, a great empire would be destroyed. It was his empire that fell.

The best-known oracle and home of the god Apollo was at Delphi, tucked 2,800 feet above the sea on the slopes of Mount

Parnassus overlooking the northern Gulf of Corinth, and believed by the Greeks to be the physical centre of the world. It was here that both private citizens and public officials came to hear their fate delivered through a chief priestess called the Pythia. The Temple of Apollo marks the spot where she sat trance-like on a tripod, breathing fumes from the narrow mouth of the chasm like any glue-sniffing teenager, and passing on divine messages.

Direct prophesies took place only on the seventh day of each month. People from all over Greece queued to submit written questions which the priest put to the Pythia, who had fasted before sitting on the tripod as Apollo's mouthpiece. Chanting in a voice altered by the hallucinatory state induced by chewing laurel leaves and inhaling the vapours, probably methane or ethylene in water bubbling up through layers of oily limestone, she relayed the answers unseen from an inner sanctum.

The story of fumes from a chasm was long thought to be a myth. However, geological surveys in the late 1990s found that the sunken sanctum was built on the foundations of a drain for a spring, which had been deliberately incorporated within the temple. There was every possibility of hallucinogenic gases rising from it, proving that the Italian poet Petrarch was correct when he described the fumes as having a very sweet perfumed smell. This is a characteristic feature of narcotic ethylene.

The oracle was also open on most other days of the month – using a simple and time-hallowed lottery of coloured broad beans. Although the precise procedure remains mysterious because it was never recorded, it seems to have worked like this. Ordinary citizens wrote and presented personal questions along a standard formula: 'Is it profitable for me to get married/risk a loan/buy a slave/plant my fields?' etc. State enquirers asked political questions along the lines: 'Is it profitable for me to invade Persia/search for the Golden Fleece/found a colony in Syracuse/destroy Athens?' The Pythia, high on ethylene, shook up the sacred lots in her bowl and then picked one out. A white bean meant 'Yes', a black bean 'No'. This random approach did not put off the questioner, who assumed the hand of Apollo to be guiding the selection. Sometimes the draw was more complex, with individual names picked from a group. The historian Plutarch, who had served as a priest at Delphi, tells how the Pythia was asked to select the king of Thessaly by drawing a bean inscribed with the successful candidate's name, though on this occasion attempts were made to rig the draw by slipping unauthorised names into her bowl.

Playing the Delphi prediction machine was not cheap. At the height of its popularity 2,400 years ago, citizens paid a fee for one draw equivalent to two days' pay, while state officials paid up to ten times as much. This early example of disguised taxation was clearly a big business, producing useful revenues. The Temple of Apollo and its surrounds must have bustled with life; today's whitened ruin full of slow-moving tourists from cruise ships is a pallid ghost of its busy and garish former self. Outside there once stood a large golden replica of the tripod, brash corporate logo and advertising sign, enticing the punters in to try their luck. It was the equivalent of the first Camelot slogan, 'It Could Be You'.

CONGRATULATIONS, YOU'VE WON A HOUSE PET

2

ROMAN EMPERORS

Rome may not have been built in a day, but it was mainly built from the proceeds of lotteries which often took place during the festivities in honour of the god Saturn. As in Greece, the seed for the idea was sown in early religious rituals when small oak rods, tiles or plates bearing inscriptions were used for oracle sessions; one was selected and the inscription interpreted to provide an answer to the question put forward.

This was later developed so that the player, upon paying the oracle a fee, drew a prize, good or bad. Sometimes a boy mixed tablets prior to drawing them out of a chest, water-filled urn or pool. According to Cicero, the whole system of divining the future this way was nothing more than an early con trick whereby Roman wideboys made a fortune by fleecing the naïve.

Using lotteries as a means of raising revenue to rebuild Rome, badly damaged after twenty years of savage civil war, came naturally to Augustus (31 BC–AD 14), the first Roman emperor. He was temperamentally wedded to chance, fate and superstition. Frightened of thunder and lightning, he carried a piece of sealskin as an amulet for protection and acted on dreams. One moved him to sit on the road once a year holding out his hand for change like any beggar on the Strand.

Augustus always believed in lots. When after a battle a father and son pleaded for their lives, he told them to draw lots to decide which of the two should be spared. The father sacrificed his life for his son, and was executed. Then the son committed suicide. This did not deter this strict disciplinarian, in later wars, from savage reprisals if one of his companies broke ranks; he would force any survivors to draw lots, and executed every tenth man. He treated civilians, however, with much greater clemency; once, as a judge, he saved a man who had killed his father from an unimaginable death by being sewn up in a sack with a dog, a cockerel, a snake and a monkey and thrown into the River Tiber. As emperor, he devised an ingenious scheme to reduce the Senate to 300 members selected by lot, but it proved too complicated and was abandoned.

A natural gambler and womaniser, Augustus played dice all his life. In a letter to his stepson Tiberius, he wrote:

> We gambled like old men through the meal, and until yesterday turned into today. Anyone who threw the Dog – two aces – or a six, put a silver piece in the pool for each of the dice; and anyone who threw Venus – when each of the dice shows a different number – scooped the lot.

And to his daughter Julia, he once wrote:

> Enclosed please find two and a half gold pieces in silver coin; which is the sum I give each of my dinner guests in case they feel like dicing or playing odd and even at table.

So it is scarcely surprising that he used games of chance to repair Rome. They took place during festivities and often during his frequent but very formal dinner parties. Unlike the later famous and notoriously extravagant feasts, these dinners were fairly restrained affairs, with low-key entertainment by musicians, acrobats or professional story-tellers. A master of ceremonies was appointed on the throw of a dice.

The games jollied things up a bit. Whimsically, he varied the value of the gifts. They could be rich clothing, gold or silver plate, or every kind of coin, including some from the early Roman monarchy or valuable foreign coinage. Or they could just be lengths of goat hair, cloth, a sponge, poker or pair of tongs, and all given in return for tokens inscribed with misleading descriptions of the objects concerned, such as 'things for dining' or 'things for the Forum'.

At dinner parties, Augustus also auctioned tickets for prizes of deliberately unequal value, including paintings with their faces turned to the wall. Every guest was expected to put in large blind bids; refusing to do so was a career, even life-limiting option. The punter might win really valuable prizes or, more likely, throw away money 'quicker than boiled asparagus', as Augustus put it. The after-prize proceeds helped the upkeep of public buildings and roads, built aqueducts and also helped to clean up the Tiber and finance the distribution of grain. Ruined or burnt temples were restored and many basilicas and public buildings of all kinds were built; this investment in Rome's infrastructure also provided many construction jobs in a city where the rate of unemployment was soaring. A single donation to the Temple of Jupiter on the Capitoline Hill consisted of 16,000 lb of gold, besides pearls and precious stones worth 500,000 gold pieces. The Palatine Temple of Apollo also benefited, as well as a great brand new Forum, dominated by the Temple of Avenging Mars built to cope with the huge increase in the number of lawsuits caused by the corresponding increase in population.

Up to the time of Augustus the city of Rome was at the mercy of fire and river floods and had been ravaged by civil war. With the help of the lucky draw, the first known public lottery for a civic cause, Augustus could justifiably boast 'I found Rome built of sun-dried bricks; I leave her clothed in marble.'

Nero (AD 54–68), great-great-grandson of Augustus and most theatrical of Roman emperors, was another lottery addict. He enlivened his spectacular feasts for the nobility with prizes of slaves, ships, villas and land and, to introduce the element of chance, prizes of dung or, if you were particularly unlucky, a spot of torture. He also used it as a method of distributing gifts to the mob, giving up to 1,000 prizes a day. Crowds scrambled for the articles, appropriately called 'missilia', as they were flung from a stage. Goods such as oil, wine and food that could not be thrown were distributed by pieces of metal or wooden balls inscribed with the names of prizes. This traditionally took place during the Great Festival, a series of plays celebrating his intention of reigning forever, which featured spectacles bizarre even by Nero's surrealistic standards, such as races between four-camel chariots and famous Roman knights riding elephants down sloping tight-ropes. Prizes could be extremely valuable. According to Suetonius they included:

> 1,000 assorted birds daily, and quantities of food parcels; besides vouchers for corn, clothes, gold, silver, precious stones, pearls, paintings, slaves, transport animals, and even trained wild beasts – and finally for ships, blocks of City tenements and farms.

Those in receipt of allegedly house-trained lions or tigers might, however, feel they had drawn the short straw.

Like Augustus, Nero was highly superstitious and just as attracted to chance as a means of deciding outcomes. If one of his armies was defeated, every tenth man was flogged to death; those who fought bravely having to draw lots along with everyone else. His more benign draws in Rome were conducted on a huge and colourful scale reflecting his histrionic, hysterical personality and love of performing. On one occasion during the second five-yearly Neronian Games he both recited poems and appeared as a musician. No-one was allowed to leave the theatre during his performances, whatever the reason. This resulted in women in the stalls giving birth, and men, driven demented by boredom, escaping by pretending to have died and being carted off for burial. They knew better than to offend their mad emperor.

Lotteries became an integral part of his great feasts, which lasted from noon to midnight. His table manners deteriorated rapidly; he would often urinate into a chamber pot and then wipe his hands on the head of a slave. This behaviour contrasted oddly with the luxurious and opulent surroundings which featured chance as a main entertainment.

In his comic masterpiece the *Satyrica*, Petronius, arbiter of elegance at Nero's court, describes the use of a wooden hen; its wings spread out into a circle as when hatching eggs, while guests searched through the straw. Some found just eggs, others artificial eggs containing gold nuggets. For the performers, life was chancy; all depended on the emperor's mood. On one occasion an acrobat slipped and bespattered Nero with food. Instead of being stripped and flogged or, even worse, fed to the alligators, he was given his freedom. The twisted logic here was that, by doing so, no-one could say that the emperor could have been bespattered by a lowly slave. So the feasts were not just a lottery for invited guests, but the entertainers, too.

The Emperor Domitian (AD 81–96), so paranoid that the pillars of his palace were made of reflective white marble so he could see what was happening behind his back, made Roman aristocrats take part in lotteries as a way of humiliating them. Forcing them to scramble for 500 lottery tickets thrown into the stands they occupied at the gladiatorial games (where a speciality was women fighting dwarves) was a control mechanism to help him cow them from plotting against him. Another method of intimidation was bullying at dinner parties, where demeaning lottery draws also took place and where everything was black, including the serving equipment, in order to frighten the guests. In a sadistic ploy those who were treated genially were often most at risk; they were the ones most likely to be crucified the next day.

Even madder than Nero was the teenage emperor Elagabalus (AD 218–222), elevated at the age of fourteen. Probably the most decadent of all the emperors, he fantasised about being a female prostitute, yearned to have a vagina sewn into his body, and specialized in sick practical jokes such as letting loose hundreds of poisonous snakes among the dawn crowds awaiting entrance to the games. Another favourite jape was to arrange for his pet lions and leopards to jump up suddenly among the guests lying on couches at his feasts, causing panic among those who did not realise they were tamed and harmless.

He extended this 'humour' to lotteries, introducing much greater variety and developing still further the element of chance. During his annual festivities, and at his own expense, he threw tickets to the crowds roaming the Roman streets which entitled the bearer to slaves, eunuchs, camels, ships and villas, or weird prizes such as ten lettuces, ten dormice or nothing at all, for many tickets were blanks.

At dinner parties, guests were presented with spoons inscribed with prizes which read 'ten ostriches', 'ten camels' or 'ten bears' (where would you put them?) or 'ten pounds of gold', 'ten pounds of lead' or 'ten dead flies'. One of his refinements was that some of the spoons, which were always distributed haphazardly, actually obliged the holder to pay ten pounds of gold, etc. 'So some rich people became poor and some poor people became rich', according to a contemporary saying. The entertainers had a separate lottery where they could win 100 gold pieces, 1,000 silver pieces, or 100 copper coins as a consolation prize; or, if they were unlucky, a dead dog or a pound of decayed beef.

Elagabalus, renowned for his amazing colour-coded feasts (one could be blue, another green), was particularly inventive. As a prelude to twenty-two courses culminating in the game, his guests ate delicacies such as peacocks' and nightingales' tongues flavoured with cinnamon, mullets' livers, flamingos' brains and dormice baked in poppies, while lounging on silver beds scattered with lilies, hyacinths and narcissi and wiped their hands on the curly hair of the young boys fanning them. At the same time, according to a possibly apocryphal story, ingenious devices in the roof cascaded such enormous quantities of violets or roses on them that on occasions some were suffocated. Those who survived drew lots.

Roman lotteries were not simply the playthings of the emperors. They were held among the Roman legions, with goods as prizes. They also selected individuals for specific posts. Before 500 BC, a small water pitcher with a sprout was used to decide an administrator from among a handful of candidates. This was swung about until a lot appeared at the spout. When dozens were in the field a large urn with a fixed revolving base was filled with water. Wooden balls, 'made as equal in size and weight as possible', according to an early inscription, were placed inside. They flew out as the vessel was spun round. But, as it was then impossible to make the balls absolutely equal in weight, the presiding magistrate could easily rig the draw. Any balls lighter than the rest, either because they were slightly smaller or were made of lighter wood, would float higher in the water, and so were far more likely to pop out of the vessel first. At a time when bribery was rampant an unscrupulous magistrate, in collusion with the operator putting in the balls, was easily able to influence the result. Scandals about officials cheating in the lottery were common.

By 30 BC, some Roman magistrates, jurors, and provincial proconsuls were randomly selected. So were some of the Vestal Virgins, though many parents went to great lengths to try and keep their daughters' names off the list of candidates; understandably, since the penalty for letting the sacred flame go out was to be buried alive. Lotteries also decided which armies the consuls should command.

Germanic tribes, traditional enemies of the Romans, also used lots. 'For auspices and the casting of lots they have the highest possible regard', records the Roman historian Tacitus. According to him, German youths were so obsessed with throwing dice that they played, sober, for hours,

> and are so recklessly keen about winning or losing that, when everything else is gone they stake their personal liberty on the last decisive throw. The loser goes into slavery without complaint; younger and stronger he may be, but he suffers himself to be bound.

There is little evidence of lotteries in Anglo-Saxon England, though in 1036, in an inversion of the Gestapo technique of shooting one in ten, bloodthirsty King Harold Harefoot let one in ten prisoners live, by drawing lots after he had arrested them as challengers to his throne. The unlucky ones were butchered slowly, 'with blows from their spears bound as they were like swine.'

It was not until the early Middle Ages that lotteries re-emerged – as systematic financial instruments relying on the practicality of lots being drawn on a massive scale. Iraqi mathematicians and Florentine merchants led the breakthrough.

" ... SO NOW WE CAN TELL PUNTERS
WHAT THEIR CHANCES OF WINNING
REALLY ARE ! "

3

MATHEMATICIANS FROM MESOPOTAMIA

If the Arab mathematician and astronomer Muhammad ibn Musa al-Khwarizmi had not promoted the concept of the zero in the ninth century AD, lotteries would never have taken off. Roman numerals severely limited the number of tickets it was possible to issue.

Arabic numbers, based on abstract mathematics and not on a system of literal counting, changed everything. For when 0 is put together with 1 it forms a binary code of whole numbers which is the basis for the operation of all calculators and computers – and for the production of an infinite number of lottery tickets.

The Romans had no alternative but to make up one new symbol after another; they used L for 50, C for 100, D was 500 and M was 1,000. A three-quarter frame round an old symbol such as D increased its value by a factor of 100,000. But they still lacked zero, which stood for no number at all. So it is as well their lotteries for prizes at games and banquets required only hundreds of tickets.

By contrast, the Greeks seemed to be aware of zero from the third century BC when they adopted it from the Babylonians. Kept under wraps in Athens because of philosophical worries about nothingness being introduced into an otherwise rational universe, the concept was later exported to India which, in turn, sent it back to Iraq. At about the same time the Mayan civilisation (300 BC–900 AD) on the isolated Yucatan peninsula also appears to have developed a zero. One symbol for this was a tattooed man in a necklace with his head thrown back; there was also a Mayan death god who represented zero and who played a role in savage ritualistic deaths, providing early evidence of its association with black magic. Probably, zero was thought up independently in a number of civilisations.

It was left to the Baghdad scholar to make practical use of the mysterious non-number, using it to revolutionise mathematics which later powered applications including architecture, astronomy, medicine, hi-tech developments and the ubiquitous internet.

Arab traders travelling the Silk Road brought this major mathematical advance to the West. By AD 1100, the new numbering was familiar among Moorish academics in Spain and in Sicily where the Normans minted a coin dated '1134 Annoy Domini' [sic], the first known example of the system in use. But this 'dangerous Saracen magic', which spread very slowly, was not welcomed; in 1299, the city of Florence banned Arabic numerals in commercial transactions. It was also forbidden to use them when entering amounts of money in trading account ledgers. There were practical reasons for insisting sums must be written out in words; Roman numerals could not easily be falsified whereas a zero could quickly be turned into a 6 or a 9 by a skilled forger.

The nub of the resistance, which continued until the early 1500s, seems to have been a fear in such a hierarchical society as medieval Italy that zero, representing the intellectually difficult and disturbing idea of nothingness, could somehow encourage disorder, if not chaos. For a period, only universities dared to experiment with it; even when Arabic numerals began to be stamped on coins, banks were reluctant to use the new system of numbering. They remained deeply suspicious of the thought that a digit's value could be changed by simply moving its place, which is how the binary system works.

As trade grew, zero became more and more popular with merchants who needed careful calculations and precise records of transactions; one advantage was zero being the balancing point of debt and credit in the then revolutionary method of double-entry bookkeeping invented in Italy some time before 1340. Even though as late as 1494, the mayor of Frankfurt instructed his accountants 'to abstain from calculating with digits', Arabic numerals were always going to triumph over tally-sticks, the abacus or simply counting on fingers.

Lotteries benefited. In the early Middle Ages they began to reappear as small private affairs conducted by churches or guilds. In thirteenth-century Brussels, market space was allocated by lottery. Their re-emergence on a more systematic scale originated in Italy with the early use of the lucky draw by Florentine merchants to encourage the sale of surplus stock. For a small sum a person drew a number from 'a jar of fortune' which entitled the holder to the article to which the number referred. However, shopkeepers making excessive profits by inflating the price of their goods and putting in too many blank tickets forced the authorities to ban the practice. It was reinstated under strict supervision and, liberated from the restrictions of Roman numerals, the enterprising merchants were able to expand the scope of the draw dramatically by issuing an ever larger number of lottery tickets. The invention of moveable type printing in the mid-fifteenth century also greatly helped.

Slowly, the use of lotteries on a large scale to raise public revenues became firmly established in Europe. By the middle of the fifteenth century they were particularly popular in the Low Countries. Records for 1443–49 show that in Ghent, Utrecht and Bruges they were mainly organised by magistrates and raised money for charities and municipal projects such as walls, fortifications and city gates. In the early Brugeois lotteries, prizes included official jobs such as wine-tasters and porters. You paid a fee to enter, and got a consolation cash prize if your ticket failed to come up. By the year 1500, jewellery-encrusted goblets, gilded silver cups, spoons, jugs and plates were commonly given in the first stirrings of the consumer society national lottery. Antwerp was famed for holding lotteries on a huge scale, printing hundreds of thousands of tickets for an extraordinary range of prizes including velvet draperies, cabinets and fine clothing. The Dutch city of Middleburg, confounding the prevailing Calvinist ethos, equalled this with a lottery whose official prize catalogue ran to eighty-three pages.

The Low Country lotteries, carefully regulated to prevent fraud, were organised so that each player received a ticket. The counterfoil, carrying that player's lucky motto, was placed with others in an urn from which they were drawn, in public, against prizes or blanks (tickets worth nothing). Unlicensed lotteries were outlawed and the game became more systematic, with the number and price of tickets as well as the number and value of prizes fixed in advance, and all sub-divided into categories (first, second, third, etc.). These were the so-called 'class' lotteries which freed the operator of risk and paved the way for state lotteries such as the one Amsterdam held in 1549 for building a church steeple.

City states in Italy were early and enthusiastic pioneers of random choice. They believed that assemblies and public offices chosen by lottery voting would automatically be proportionally more representative, harder to gerrymander and be more receptive. In Verona, as early as the thirteenth century, all paid offices were elected by lot. In Venice, the election of the Doge, the republic's lifetime leader, took five days in a complicated system which started with thirty names being drawn from an urn containing several hundred names of prominent families. There followed five separate lotteries for selecting groups which then did the actual election. This complex device of alternate 'lottery draws' and elections was designed to prevent factional strife, and lasted until 1797. Risk-taking Venetian merchants, Europe's most powerful traders throughout the fifteenth century, also took financial lotteries to their hearts. They were seen as a new way of financing and of redistributing wealth, with prizes of silver, jewellery and precious stones being presented to the ringing of church bells, at grand public spectacles in Venice's squares. They also provided income for convents and churches.

In Florence, the city government was appointed bi-monthly by lot although, as a safeguard against incompetence, candidates were first carefully scrutinised and approved. Genoa followed suit in the sixteenth century, annually filling five key political positions from among the ninety members of the Senate. Its citizens were so taken with this novel idea that they began making side bets on the results, inspiring the senate to set up a financial lottery on the same principle. Its popularity inspired many other Italian cities, including Florence, Milan, Bologna, Turin and Naples, to imitate it, offering prizes not only in goods but also in money.

Not all lotteries in Renaissance Italy were welcomed. When the Pope set up a lottery in Rome to increase the revenues for the Church, Romans became so addicted to it that many families went without food and clothes to finance the stake money. Centuries later, in 1860, visitors to Rome complained that no gambling other than the Papal lottery was permitted; each year, it sold an astonishing fifty-five million tickets to a population of less than 200,000. One described advertisements as 'gay, parti-coloured stripes of paper, inscribed with the cabalistic figure', that were being flaunted at every street corner. Another reported that at the regular saturday draw in the Piazza Madonna, some players held a crucifix in their right hand and a lottery ticket in the left and would often 'let the Ticket make contact with the crucifix as if kissing it.' The Papal lottery did good though; Pope Clement XII (1730–1740) used it to finance well-known landmarks, including that tourist favourite, the baroque masterpiece the Trevi Fountain.

One game developed in fifteenth-century Italy was called *blanca carta* after the white colour of blank tickets, which far exceeded the winning tickets which were all numbered. When Francois I of France took up the idea of lotteries from the Italians in 1520, he also adapted the name, allowing the game by edict under the brand of Blanques. From 1539 he authorised a number of lotteries on condition that the operators paid a levy to the state. From 1563 to 1609, the French Parliament repeatedly tried to ban them. However, in Paris in 1572 and again in 1588, Louis de Gonzague, Duke of Nivernois, established lotteries with the blessing of Pope Sextus V for giving marriage dowries to young women working on his estates.

English merchants trading in the Low Countries and Italy would have been aware of the way the lucky draw was spreading across Europe. They almost certainly imported the idea into England.

WITH RESPECT, MA'AM, YOUR SUBJECTS
THINK THIS IS VIRGIN ON THE RIDICULOUS

4

IT COULD BE YE

The first Elizabethans did not need Camelot's chief executive officer, Dianne Thompson, to warn them: 'it probably won't be you.' They quickly worked out for themselves that odds of 1 in 16,000 in winning Queen Elizabeth I's great lottery of 1568 – England's first – were stacked too high, and they abstained en masse from playing – much to her embarrassment since she had hoped to raise enough money to repair the nation's dilapidated harbours. Today's lottery odds of 1 in 14 million would have been totally beyond their comprehension.

Yet, at the time, it must have seemed an ingenious wheeze to Sir William Cecil, arch flatterer, manipulator and principal secretary of state to Elizabeth, in one of the most extraordinary personal and professional partnerships in English history. It had been a good ten years for Cecil, the original Sir Humphrey. He had craftily so extended the powers of the office of secretary that he was now able to interfere in virtually everything from top level international diplomacy to increasing the amount of fish in the national diet. With his support the young Queen, spirited and highly intelligent though disconcertingly capricious on occasion, had made an excellent start. Since her coronation in 1559, England had enjoyed relative peace and prosperity. Compared with the revolts in the Netherlands and the increasingly fierce conflicts in France, governing the nation had been reasonably smooth. And Cecil could justifiably take much of the credit.

However, the outlook was darkening. Events in Europe were starting to impact, seriously disrupting England's cloth trade, which comprised two-thirds of its exports and underwrote tens of thousands of jobs. Anglo-Spanish relations were fast deteriorating, the Irish wars were beginning to cost too much, and in the Channel, English pirates were ever bolder in threatening trade.

Rebuilding the navy and the merchant fleet was vital, in tandem with the need to restore the ports. Some, like Ramsgate and Sandwich, had declined dramatically due to the sea receding and rivers silting up; harbour mouths became blocked. Calais had been lost to the French a decade earlier, while its counterpoint Dover, the best naval base on the Channel, needed to unblock and repair its superb coastal harbour.

Mismanagement was rife. So poor was Winchelsea that it could not pay its share of the wages of the bailiffs the Cinque Ports used to regulate fisheries; Romney and Sandwich defaulted on upkeep payments and their mayors were threatened with imprisonment. Squabbles soared. A General Brotherhood (the assembly of the Cinque Ports) held at Romney records that serjeants at law had to adjudicate on many 'fynes, contemptes, stryves, variaunceis, contencions, douttes, questions, debates, varieties, and ambiguities'.

So it was clear to Cecil that resources were needed to improve the ports and their management at a time when sea power and trade were key to England's prosperity and defence. But how to raise the money? None could be provided by taxation. Parliament, determined to keep England the lowest-taxed nation in Europe, would approve expenditure only at times of real crisis. Nor could any be got from further loans on the Antwerp money market since interest rates there had already soared to an exorbitant fourteen per cent. None could be provided from the Queen's own income, since she always overspent it. No wonder Cecil complained: 'lack of money is the principal sickness in this Court.'

Fortunately, his genius lay in dreaming up innovative ways of funding unusual expenditure. Already, in order to pay German mining experts from Augsburg to work mines in the Lake District, he had introduced the then revolutionary idea of a one penny tax on each household, the so-called 'Peter's Pence.'

He looked overseas for inspiration and found it across the North Sea in England's mirror image: the Low Countries. English merchants trading there reported that cities such as Ghent, Utrecht, Antwerp and Bruges had developed a particularly clever method of raising public revenues for building fortifications and other municipal projects: a lottery.

By quizzing traders who had seen it operate, Cecil became convinced the idea would work for England, but then he had the unenviable task of convincing Elizabeth, who was suspicious. In this, she resembled another strong-willed female leader who, four centuries on, was to entertain doubts about another national lottery in the United Kingdom: Margaret Thatcher. It took all of Cecil's guile and obsequious charm to persuade the reluctant monarch.

Eventually, she agreed; on 23 August 1567, a Royal Proclamation was published, heralded as 'A VERY RICH LOTTERIE GENERALL WITHOUT ANY BLANCKES.' The proceeds were for 'the reparation of the havens [harbours] and the strength of the realme and towards such other publique good workes.' Posters five feet high and twenty inches wide advertising ticket prices and showing off the prizes were displayed prominently on walls and doors around the City of London.

But the lottery was not popular; the public simply did not trust it. Optimistically, it was hoped that 400,000 tickets would be sold at ten shillings each to yield a net profit of £100,000 for harbour repairs. The plan was to give nearly 30,000 prizes of a total value of about £55,000, returning to each of the 370,000 unlucky players half a crown, or twety-five per cent of their original bet. The first prize was £5,000 (an attractive £100,000 in today's money) split £3,000 in cash, £700 in gold and silver plate, and the remainder in good tapestry and the highest quality linen. The second prize was £3,500 (£70,000 today) divided into £2,000 in money, £600 in plate and the rest in tapestry and linen. There were eleven more premier prizes declining in value to £140 and then various others from £100 to 14 shillings. In addition, the very first person to draw a winning ticket got a 'Welcome', a bonus of silver gilt plate worth £50, and the next two 'Welcomes' of silver plate each worth £30 and £20 respectively.

Foreigners were enticed to take part by only having to pay half the export duties on goods won or goods purchased with money prizes, though given the notoriously corrupt and chaotic customs system of the day, they could probably have got away with paying nothing. The Dutch benefited the most.

Other ingenious incentives were offered such as the freedom from arrest for a seven-day period for criminals coming into the larger towns to buy tickets, though those charged with major crimes such as murder, treason or piracy were not eligible. Guaranteed safe conduct may have been the theory, but in practice it did not work for those naïve enough to trust the amnesty. A State official called I. Aldaye wrote to Cecil on April 30 1569:

> A prisoner in the Counter [one of five prisons in Southwark] for debt. Thought he should have been protected under the Proclamation for the Lottery, but it was made a jest of.

Tickets were available in the City of London from the Feast of St Bartholomew (24 August, 1567) and also in York, Norwich, Exeter, Lincoln, Coventry, Southampton, Hull, Bristol, Newcastle, Chester, Ipswich, Salisbury, Oxford, Cambridge, Shrewsbury, Dublin and Waterford. In a shrewd move, the Proclamation was sent out in the

targeted counties by officials such as Justices of the Peace and sheriffs. Cecil knew most of them personally. They were instructed to
set up boards of collectors and promised that for every pound collected in ticket sales the chief collector would be given sixpence to
be split among his assistants. It was made very clear that their job
was to sell as many tickets as possible to ordinary members of the
public. Approaches were made to the 3,500 Merchant Adventurers
who ran the cloth trade from ports along the east and south coasts
and who represented the bulk of England's exporters. Members of
this government-backed body living in Antwerp were also asked
for support, through a special agent called George Gilpin.

Even at this stage, Elizabeth was uneasy. This can be deduced
from the letter's threat to arrest, try and punish for slander anyone
who spread stories that the money was for her own private use.

From the start, support was low; even the Irish, belying their
reputation as a gambling nation, bought tickets worth less than
£500. The length of time between the initial sale of the tickets
from 24 August 1567 (the latest day for buying was 15 April 1568
for the country, 1 May for London) and the draw due on 25 June
1568 was a huge disadvantage. Later lotteries were careful not to
repeat this mistake. Players were also so confused over precisely
when the draw would take place that on 13 September 1567 the
lord mayor of London had to issue his own proclamation promising that the draw would not be postponed beyond June 1568
without 'very greate and urgent cause.' He spoke too soon. The
ill-fated draw had to be put off several times by royal proclamation in the vain hope that enough tickets would eventually be
sold. So few were taking part that on 3 January 1568 the Queen
issued another proclamation postponing the draw on the grounds
that the money collectors had not received their instructions in
good time, on account of some being ill, others having died, and
others being too busy with their public duties.

At first, Cecil was convinced that a major propaganda campaign to persuade boroughs, towns and villages to enter would
do the trick. Lacking the resources and techniques of today's mass

media and the services of spin doctors, he decided to send a body of twenty surveyors backed by treasurers, collectors and hundreds of constables to tour the country and whip up enthusiasm. This operation was to be masterminded by a surveyor of the lottery, appointed with strict instructions to ensure 'that ther shall not one parishe escape but they bring in some money into the Lottes.' The campaign opened on 12 July 1568 with a circular, probably one of the first direct mailshots in history, being sent to all Justices of the Peace, treasurers, mayors, sheriffs, bailiffs, constables and lottery collectors already appointed in Kent, Sussex, Surrey, Southampton and the Isle of Wight.

This urged them to sell more tickets. Initially, the surveyor, wielding an iron fist beneath a velvet glove, seemed to be making progress. A number of municipalities paid up. Even Yarmouth, traditionally independent, bought two blocks of tickets each worth £15. Its motto read:

> Yermouth haven, God send thee spede
> The Lord he knoweth thy great need

Another deserving port, Hastings, also subscribed, stating hopefully:

> From Hastings we come
> God send us good speed
> Never a poor fisher town in England
> Of ye great lot hath more need

Rather louchely, Brighton declared:

> Draw Brightemston a good lot
> Or else return them a turbot

The lord mayor of London, who bought thirty tickets, said simply: 'God preserve the Cytye of London.'

Despite the best efforts of this Queen's army of surveyors *et al*, the scheme continued to be viewed with the deepest suspicion by Elizabeth's not so loyal subjects, who remained untempted by the beautiful silver and gold plate on display as prizes at London houses such as that of the Queen's goldsmith and engraver to the Mint, Antony Derick.

These dazzling exhibitions helped to encourage contributions from City livery companies. Towns, public bodies and individual Justices of the Peace and sheriffs also bought tickets as a civic duty. The public, convinced they were being diddled, did not. So many books of tickets had not been returned that Elizabeth had to proclaim another postponement until 11 January 1569. The draw itself was a farce, the sixteenth-century equivalent of *Carry On Up The Lottery*.

It took place in a timber and board lottery house built against the wall near the west door of old St Paul's Cathedral. Although as dilapidated as any of the harbours, it was an appropriately raucous and raffish venue for a lucky draw. Lackadaisical senior clergy had allowed the whole area to be degraded into a mix of public market, street carnival and promenade ground for Elizabethan fashion victims.

Money-lenders operated in the south aisle, horses were sold in the nave and servants waited to be hired at a central pillar. Choir boys swarmed 'like so many white butterflies' around gallants entering the building to demand an entrance fee. Porters carrying beer casks and great baskets of fruit, fish and bread, butchers, water-bearers and colliers with sacks of coal used the nave as a shortcut, while horses and mules were often led through the building. The font served as a convenient meeting place for settling debts and making payments; St Dunstan's chapel had become a glass storehouse and parts of the crypt had been colonised by stationers and trunk-makers whose constant banging and knocking disturbed church services. Drunks and beggars slept on the pews, urinating and defecating where they lay; it was 'veryye lothsome to beholde.'

Outside, it was worse. Brawling, and the drawing of swords was common. Archers practised longbow and crossbow shooting using the cathedral's external statues as target practice. Hoodies of the day threw stones at the pigeons, crows and jackdaws, further vandalising the semi-ruined parapets which towered over the square mile of narrow streets just up from the River Thames.

It was in this circus-like atmosphere – Cecil, control freak that he was, must have hated it – that the draw, preceded by a trumpeter, began on 11 January 1569. The process was laborious, long-drawn out and continued 'daie and night' for four months until 6 May.

Delays were inevitable. Because one twelfth only of the £400,000 had been collected, under the terms of the original scheme, the prize list had to be reduced to about £9,000 instead of rather more than £100,000. So, under this system, the first prize winner could expect to receive only four hundred and sixteen pounds, thirteen shillings and four pence (being a twelfth of the £5,000 top prize). On the other hand, the number of chances given to each ticket was increased in inverse proportion to the reduction of prize money. This meant the name of each player of ten shillings was placed twelve times in the lottery wheel containing the counterfoils. Thus in one wheel 400,000 counterfoils were placed, inscribed with the players' names and mottos. In the other were placed 29,505 prize tickets bearing one twelfth of the original value, together with 370,495 blanks. The problem was to match the two sets of tickets because each had to be drawn by hand from the two wheels. Some livery companies became suspicious and despatched representatives to attend the draw in twenty-four-hour shifts.

Attempts were made to liven up these tedious proceedings through a device similar to that used in the Low Countries. In order to conceal the identities of ticket-holders, jocular remarks had been written instead of names on the counterfoils of the sold tickets. These were read out to jeers and cheers of the crowd, swilling ale and munching pies baked by an enterprising entrepreneur in an oven cheekily dug into a nearby buttress. They were the progenitors of the joking TV personality presenting the weekly results of the UK National Lottery.

Protestants assembled there would have surely applauded, 'In God I hope and a fart for the Pope', contribution of William Seintleger of Canterbury, who held ticket number 230,364.

Everyone must have been baffled by Thomas Watson of Cirencester, ticket number unrecorded, who had written the decidedly enigmatic motto, 'The head of a snake with garlic is good meat.'

Annam Waldegrave of Buris, ticket number 343,775, was refreshingly straightforward with her 'Seeing shillings ten, shall thousands win/Why should I fear to them in.'

Desperation clearly crept into the offering from William Dorghtie de Westholme, ticket number 193,315, who implored:

God send a great lot for my children and me,
Which have had twenty by one wife truly.

The lottery was not a success. Despite everything, it sold fewer than 34,000 tickets at ten shillings each instead of the 400,000 originally planned and raised less than £5,000 instead of the £100,000 envisaged. No-one seems to have won very much. The Drapers contributed £54 and received in return some undistinguished pieces of armour which, not being soldiers, they could not use. Sportingly, they gave a two-shilling tip to the lottery house porter and sixpence to the servant who brought the useless breastplates to their hall. The only person who benefitted, if a report filed by the French Ambassador, Monsieur de la Motte Fenelon, is to be believed, was the Queen herself. According to him, she withdrew a large sum of the prize money for her own use shortly before the draw. As she always found it impossible to live within her income despite frequent investigations by auditors, people believed the slander.

As for rebuilding the ports, an emergency twelve-month loan had to be raised from London merchants via the Privy Council.

Future repairs, including the modernisation of Dover harbour, relied on bizarre schemes such as charging a two shilling and six-pence fee for all new licences for the nation's taverns.

Although Elizabeth never launched another public lottery, twenty years later she rewarded the lord mayor with 'bason and ewre' for organising a private one. Some livery companies such as the Drapers, distrustful on account of the 1569 debacle, did not subscribe. Its purpose is not known, but this time great care was taken to run the event honestly and efficiently, with 'cer-taine psonnes of credite and trust.' The draw, held at the Lottery House in St Paul's churchyard in June 1585, was witnessed by many respectable City men, including three witnesses from the Merchant Taylors' Livery Company. It took just four hours, from 8am to noon, instead of the four months of the port's lottery. It was not free from controversy.

Five years later, Sir Richard Sherborne, Lord Lieutenant, Lancashire JP and secret Papist, was charged with an amazing variety of crimes including adultery, incest, threatening to hang constables, never lending money to the Queen and 'retaining sundry sums due to people on the end of the last lottery.'

For the remainder of Elizabeth's reign lotteries were out of fashion; a quarter of a century later they were to play a crucial role in an event that changed the world.

That must be last week's lotto winner

5

SAVING VIRGINIA

In 2007 the United States and the United Kingdom commemorated the founding, 400 years earlier, of England's first permanent settlement in America – at Jamestown, in a wilderness called Virginia named in honour of Queen Elizabeth the First, the Virgin Queen. Her namesake, Queen Elizabeth the Second, and the United States President George W. Bush travelled to the Jamestown site where they both spoke enthusiastically of the way the settlement had laid the foundations for the rule of law, free enterprise and representative government, as well as the politically correct 'cultural diversity.' Much was made of the historic four-and-a-half-month voyage across treacherous seas of three tiny English ships, *Susan Constant*, *Godspeed* and *Discovery*, and their eventual safe landing at Jamestown in May 1607. But the 400th anniversary of the dawning of the New World was a close call.

In its early days the finances of the settlement were worse than Enron's, the land was proving virtually impossible to clear, disease was spreading, wars with the Algonquian Indians led by the charismatic chief, Powhatan, were increasing, and there were not enough stores. The combination of all these misfortunes threatened to wreck the work of the planters, who had set sail so optimistically in search of a new life an ocean away from the religious and class intolerance of England. Not all of the colonists were so high minded.

The private Virginia Company, set up under licence from the Crown to establish 'a colonie of sondrie of our people into that parte of America', was becoming desperate and saw lotteries as a quick way to finance Jamestown. It first tried a scheme which was marketed to London merchants as a double whammy. This was designed to rid the streets of the City of London of aggressive beggars, 12,000 by one estimate, and also asylum seekers by transporting them as human resources to the new colony.

By 1600, 4,000 people in London out of a population of 100,000 were foreigners. Many of them had fled in boatloads from Catholic massacres and persecution in France and the Low Countries where England became known as the 'Asylum Christi.' Then, as now, the local population objected to the pressure this influx of aliens put on jobs, shelter and health care, such as it was. In addition, many unemployed and homeless from the countryside had flocked to the expanding capital in search of a living. An Act passed in 1598 for the Punishment of Rogues, Vagabonds and Sturdy Beggars had little impact on the bands of ruffians who haunted Cheapside and elsewhere, annoying and intimidating the citizens.

So, early in 1609 the Virginia Company sent a notice, endorsed by the lord mayor of London, to all City livery companies appealing for funds 'to ease the City and Suburbs of a swarme of unnecessary inmates, as a continual cause of dearth and famine, and the very originall cause of all the plagues.' It asked for 'some voluntary contribucon for their remove into this Plantacon of

Virginia, which wee understand you all seemeth to like as an action pleasing to God.'

What if the beggars and refugees refused to exchange the streets of London for the wilds of North America? The Virginia Company had a ready answer. Their notice to the Merchant Taylors' Company of 7 March 1609 suggested the colony be presented in a way that makes the average Spanish time-share salesman look like George Washington:

> And if the inmates called before you and enjoined to remove, shall alleadge he hath not place to remove unto, but must lye in the streets, and, being offred to go this journey, shall demaund what may be theire present maintenance, what may be theire future hopes, it maye please you to let them knowe that for the present they shall have meate, drink and clothing, with an howse, orchard and garden.

Shares, which were sold corporately and individually, cost £12.50 (very roughly £1,700 today), £25 and £50. The Merchant Taylors responded enthusiastically. A minute, dated 29 April 1609, notes: 'Two hundred pounds shal be presently sent to Sir Thomas Smyth Tre'sorer of the Virginia Company.' Individual members contributed £587 in the names of themselves, their children or friends. Rewards were to be allocated in proportion to 'all such mines and minerals, of gould, silver, and other metals or treasure, pearles, precious stones, or any kind of wares or marchaundizes, commodities, or profits whatsoever', resulting from the voyage. Within five years, it was a different story.

The reality of life in Jamestown was far removed from the false idyll described in the propaganda sent to the livery companies. Instead of houses, gardens and orchards the settlers had to cope with dysentery and typhoid from drinking poisoned water, plagues of mosquitoes, malnutrition and hostile Indians whose women were encouraged to torture captured colonists to death by using sharp mussel shells to scrape flesh from their bones.

Flaying alive, boiling to death, and beating out of brains with large clubs were other favourite methods of execution.

The first expedition, which landed in 1607, was a strange mix of entrepreneurs looking to make their fortunes, deceived vagrants and some idealists; few among them were qualified to cultivate the land, rear livestock or build weather-proof shelters. 'A more damned crew hell never vomited,' said the president of the Virginia Company. They were also inadequately equipped and supplied partly because King James I, son of Mary Queen of Scots whom the Virgin Queen had executed for treason, gave very little financial and material support. Even though Jamestown on the River James had been named in his honour, this strange monarch took no interest in it; he believed the skies there were filled with flying squirrels, feared its barbarous savages might try to emigrate to England and regarded the tobacco plants grown there from 1612 as poisonous and smoking as 'dangerous to the lungs'. This insight, well ahead of his time, did not prevent him from taxing heavily tobacco imports from Virginia, an increasingly important source of revenue for the crown.

Lack of resources in an extreme and unfamiliar climate where crops refused to grow, where rats ate the stored sacks of corn and where sampling unknown forest berries and fungi was a deadly gamble, gradually took its toll. By 1609 the settlers were starving and eating anything they could get their hands on; acorns, roots, boots, snakes and even boiled and stewed corpses dug from graves. One man, driven mad by hunger, killed his pregnant wife, cut out and threw away their unborn child, and ate parts of her limbs before being discovered and stopped. He was burned at the stake

More than half of the 6,000 colonists starved to death, the Indians killed many others, while some, demented by the horrors they had seen, vanished into the wilderness. Only sixty of them, looking like survivors of Belsen, remained when a supply fleet from England carrying another 300 immigrants arrived in June 1610 and, just in time, stopped them from abandoning the settlement.

When news of the near-disaster eventually reached England, even King James felt obliged to help, albeit very reluctantly. This he did not by a direct grant from the Exchequer but by granting permission, in 1612, for public lotteries to be held, 'in speciall favour for the present plantation of English Colonies in Virginia.' Eight years later a privy councillor, Sir Lionel Cranfield, revealed in a letter that James said privately he 'never liked the lotterie; he ever suspected it would prove hurtful and distasteful', and had agreed to it only 'upon information that the plantation could not subsist without it.' Sir Edwin Sandys, a leading politician, entrepreneur, Puritan divine and one of the key figures in the company, led the publicity campaign which included a patriotic and politically-incorrect ballad, London's Lotterie. Sung to the tune of Lully Gallant, it trumpeted its purpose as:

> It is to plant a Kingdome sure,
> Where savadge people dwell;
> God will favour Christians still,
> And like the purpose well.

Although 60,000 tickets remained unsold in the first lottery, there was 'no abating of any prize' and the prizes consisted of £5,000 in cash and valuable plate. The draw, postponed for a month due to the death of the Lord Treasurer Robert Cecil, took place in the lottery house at St Paul's Cathedral from 29 June to 20 July, observed throughout by noblemen and gentlemen as well as 'sundry graue discreet Cittizens.' All the witnesses, both aristocrats and commoners, agreed there was fair play. Thomas Sharpcliffe, a London tailor, won first prize, 'fayre plate' worth £1,000, which was 'sent to his house in very stately manner.' The congregation of St Mary Colechurch at Old Jewry, who had bet £6 to support spreading the gospel among the American savages, did less well; they ended up with two spoons valued at £1. Some participants declined to pick up their prizes on moral grounds. Among them was Dr Laurence Chatterton, a Puritan divine and master of Emmanuel College, Cambridge, who was given a £12 50s. stake in the draw when he joined the Virginia Company that year. He later went on to live until the astonishing age of 104, no doubt receiving his reward in heaven.

Sufficient was raised to begin supporting the cost of supplying more men and, increasingly, women, munitions, body armour to deflect Indian arrows, food supplies and equipment to the beleaguered colony. Lotteries, regarded as 'the first and most certaine' way to obtain funds, eventually accounted for almost half of the yearly income of the debt-ridden Virginia Company and almost certainly saved it from tipping into bankruptcy. But by 1615, 'lottery fatigue', which was to affect all future lotteries at some stage, had begun to set in. A Privy Council declaration published in February to try and drum up support complained of 'poore and barren receipts at the Lottery house for this twelve moneth past.' The Merchant Taylors, once so supportive, could barely rustle up £50 and a clerk signed off the list of ticket holders in High Wycombe with the words 'Possibilia spes comitatus', Latin for 'Fat Chance'. There were also complaints that the poor, who could ill afford it, were seduced into playing, a familiar refrain of lottery critics over the next 400 years. Marketing was pepped up for the draw on 17 November 1615; attractive advertisements appeared featuring unthreatening looking Indians holding their bows and arrows in a rather camp manner, the value of the plate prizes was increased and there were more of them, including ornaments worth £25 for the first- and last-drawn blank tickets. If they disliked their pieces of plate, winners had the option of taking cash instead, less ten per cent of the value. Anyone spending over £3 got a spoon.

The following year the Virginia Company pulled off a spectacular publicity coup by using the Indian princess Pocahontas, daughter of Powhatan, to create interest in the draws. She arrived from Virginia in June on board the man-of-war the *Treasurer* with her husband John Rolfe, the first settler to grow tobacco as a cash crop in the colony. The exotic, fabulous-looking Pocahontas became an instant celebrity in London society; she went round with Anne of Denmark, the wife of King James, to balls and plays, an engraving of her was sold widely, and she was accommodated in the appropriately named Belle Savage, a theatre tavern situated conveniently on Ludgate Hill just yards from the lottery house at St Paul's. She met James himself on at least one occasion. A terse entry in the state archives for 18 January 1617 records, 'The Virginian woman, Pocahuntas has been with the King; she is returning home, sore against her will.' Lady Rebecca Rolfe, as she had become known, never made it; she died, probably from pneumonia, at Gravesend in March at the start of the return voyage.

'Running lotteries' travelling from town to town were also held in Bristol, Canterbury, Chester, Southampton, York and Salisbury (1616), Plymouth and Norwich (1617), Leicester and Manchester (1618) and Reading and Exeter (1619). These provincial draws, run by two able and persuasive company agents, Gabriel Barbor and the aptly named Lott Peere, were highly profitable; each paid for at least one supply ship and £29,000 was raised in total. To smooth the way, the civic authorities were routinely offered a bribe, usually between £20 and £40. For this, they were expected to find a venue, ensure tickets were kept safely under lock and key and 'well mingled together', choose a child to pick out the winning numbers and stop 'the poorer sorte' from playing. This last instruction was to deflect growing criticism that the company was encouraging poor people to buy tickets they could not afford. At the same time, a campaign was intensified to persuade English diplomats and merchants trading in the Low Countries to dip in their purses and take part. Not all were impressed. In a letter written in cipher to Phillip III, king of Spain, the Spanish ambassador to England, Don Pedro de Zuniga, denounced this wheeze to bail out their enemy's first American colony as 'a generall kind of begging.' A London merchant, Thomas Albery, warned William Trumbull, James I's agent in Brussels, 'I feare coldly for the honour of our state.' Begging or not, it did the trick.

Then, in 1620, Parliament suddenly stopped all lotteries on account of complaints from traders, almost certainly exaggerated, that the excitement had demoralised business and industry.

Internal squabbling within the Virginia company and accusations of misappropriation of funds also contributed to its demise which was announced in a Privy Council proclamation on 21 March. It explained that 'the sayd Lotteries, hauing now for a long time been put in vse, doe dayly decline to more and more inconueniences, to the hinderance of multitudes of Our Subjects.'

But by this time, greatly aided by growing tobacco exports to England, peace with the Indians and proper cultivation of the land, the increasingly self-sufficient Jamestown settlement had finally come of age. Lotteries had been the midwife to the birth of the New World. They were later to play a very significant role in helping it to grow up.

"IF IT'S A ROLLOVER WEEK, WE COULD BE FREE BY THURSDAY"

6

FREEING THE BRITISH SLAVES OF BARBARY

Many lotteries for all kinds of good causes followed the saving of Virginia, but the most bizarre has to be those which helped pay the ransoms of Britons enslaved by Barbary pirates. Between 1530 and 1780 more than one million white Europeans, men, women and children, were taken in captivity to Barbary (northern Africa from Gibraltar to Tripoli in Libya). Tens of thousands of these were British, with more than 800 English, Scottish, and Welsh cargo ships being seized in the Mediterranean and Atlantic from 1600 to 1640 alone.

It was a lucrative trade, which caused damage to English shipping totalling hundreds of millions of pounds at today's prices, while hostage-taking proved another useful revenue stream and was a huge problem. Magnify a thousand-fold the hostage-taking in Bush's war on terror and you have an idea of its scale.

From about 1625 in this earlier age of Islamophobia, Muslim pirate ships from north Africa began appearing off the British coast. Lack of Royal Naval frigates meant that Cornwall and Devon in particular were helpless in the face of Muslim privateering; every year hundreds of sailors and fishermen from large ports such as Plymouth were regularly taken at sea. Ireland, too, was at the mercy of the marauders, who in reality were mostly sea-going mercenaries systematically raising revenue for state sponsors in Morocco, Algeria and Tunisia. The small Irish village of Baltimore in County Cork was raided in 1631, its thatched roofs fired, and 109 captives transported to Algiers where the men were forced to work chained in the galleys and the women and children put in harems and brothels. Some found their sudden kidnap from sleepy countryside to a totally alien and threatening environment too much to bear and died of fright shortly after arrival in north Africa.

In 1640, four large Turkish pirate ships took sixty men, women and children from the shore near Penzance. According to a contemporary London report this happened at night, 'for in the day these rogues keep out of sight for fear of the King's ships.' Other captives among the 34,000 estimated to be held in Barbary at any one time were more fortunate. One West Countrywoman Mary Brewster, having been sold into the Sultan's harem, was redeemed from Algiers for £1,342. Six women seized from Youghall in southern Ireland years before were finally returned in 1646.

Although Parliament eventually imposed a duty on imports and exports to raise ransoms, the English state, unlike France and Spain, did little else to help their captives. It was left to churches and chapels to publicise their plight in newspapers, pamphlets, woodcuts and sermons – usually by exaggerated horror stories involving Turkish buggery, slaves being sawn in half or being whipped with dried bull's penises in the galleys – and to raise money for their release. Military action brought some home. When the Venetian Captain-General Morosini captured the Ionian island of Lefkas from the Turks on 7 August 1684, he set free 130 Christian slaves working there in the fortress of Santa Maura.

More official help was gradually forthcoming; the state donated a £50 allowance for each redemption and arranged regular national collections. Millions of pounds in today's money were raised each time, though the inevitable fraudster siphoned some off. Rich merchants, anxious to stabilise sea trade, also donated substantial sums. There were countless private appeals by relatives desperate to bring home their loved ones. Lotteries, licensed again after being banned under Cromwell, played their part. The inspiration is likely to have been a lottery in Paris organized by three ladies, with tickets at forty *sous* each, for redeeming French slaves in the Turkish galleys.

On August 7 1660 following the restoration of the monarchy that year, Captain Thomas Gardiner petitioned King Charles II 'to empower him to hold a lottery in England and Wales for three years, for ransom of English slaves at Tunis, Algiers or in the Turkish galleys or for any other charitable use.' Like so many other Royalist soldiers, the English Civil War had ruined Gardiner financially. He was taken prisoner at Newark, imprisoned for a year and, in 1657, during a plot to kill Cromwell, was captured with two loaded pistols and a dagger in the gallery of Hampton Court, where the Protector held his councils. He spent another year in jail after narrowly escaping being sentenced to death at his trial through lack of conclusive evidence.

Large-scale demobilisation of armed forces, whether American soldiers from the Vietnam conflict in the twentieth century or from the English Civil War in the seventeenth, always creates social problems. *Mercurius Publicus*, the Pravda of the day, boasted:

> The Commissioners prosecute the disbanding of the Army and Navy with all vigour and expedition day and night, to exonerate the Kingdom from future Taxes towards their pay.

The result was poverty for large numbers of unemployed former fighting men. Some, such as the maimed soldiers of Lord Cottington's lifeguard, were reduced to begging in the streets;

others were allowed, by Royal warrant, to dispose of their plate and books by lottery.

Charles was clearly a fan. When Prince Rupert of the Rhine, nephew of Charles I and charismatic commander of the Royalist cavalry died, it was decided to dispose of his jewellery, worth £20,000, by lottery. To reassure players all was in order, the King agreed that he, personally, would supervise the draw, scheduled to take place at the Banqueting Hall in Whitehall with a child appointed by him taking out the numbers. An advertisement in *The London Gazette* of 7 January 1684 announced:

> As to the fairness of the proceedings therein, as many of the Adventurers [players] as will, may be present, when the KING shall please to read the Prizes, and to put them among the Blanks.

The thought of Charles shouting out the names of the lucky winners like a bingo caller ('Eighty Nine – Charley's Fine!') is hilarious, though unfortunately I can find nothing to confirm he actually did it.

Gardiner's petition proposed that a third of the lottery profits be donated to the ransom fund, with the other two-thirds being kept by him 'for his expenses and repair of his fortunes ruined by loyalty.' Surprisingly the King, possibly pricked by conscience, agreed to this huge mark-up and granted the request. Records show that the attorney general, as was customary, drew up the necessary paperwork and written permissions, but it is not known how much money was raised. It is probable, however, that the proceeds would have helped bring back to England some of the 300 male slaves in Algiers who, in 1662, sent a petition to King Charles pleading to be redeemed. They were among an estimated 1,200 English captives held there in appalling and humiliating conditions. Some, including former merchants and one English consul, were harnessed with mules and asses to carts in the quarries and were imprisoned at night in deep pits in the ground.

Slave-taking was not, it must be said, a peculiarly Muslim activity; all the European powers operating in the Mediterranean did it. The Royal Navy regularly sold on the slave market any Muslims it captured from the Barbary States. The Journal of Sir Thomas Allin, the Royal Naval Commander at the time, is full of such transactions. A 1669 entry, for example, records his leaving with Don Quevedo en Contreras, British vice consul at Port Mahon in Minorca:

> One blind, one lame, one old Moor and one about 30 years, to be sold for his Majesty's use and bread and hog's flesh to be bought with the proceeds for the fleet.

The London Gazette routinely carried advertisements about 'Negro' slaves who had escaped from their British masters, mainly in London, offering a standard reward of two guineas a head for their capture. Neither, on occasion, did the British state itself hesitate to sell freeborn Britons as slaves; in 1656, seventy West Countrymen suspected of royalist sympathies, including a seventy-six-year-old gentleman farmer from Tiverton, were shipped to Barbados and sold to brutal planters for sugar. Three years later a petition to Parliament for their release described them as:

> Grinding at the Mills, attending the Furnaces, or digging in this scorching Island, having nothing to feed on (notwithstanding their hard labour) but Potatoe roots.

An end to the ordeal of the English slaves seemed to be in sight in 1662 when Admiral Lawson, who commanded a squadron in the Mediterranean, negotiated on behalf of King Charles a peace treaty with Algiers. It contained a special clause for their release, offering '£10,000, *at the rate they were first sold in the market*' (my italics).

Two churchmen, Dr John Bargrave and Archdeacon Sellecke of Bath were sent to Algiers with an agent general, a young man called Francis Baker (later to become Consul at Algiers) to ensure that the £10,000, including presumably the lottery's contribution, was spent properly on ransoms and not diverted elsewhere. The money secured the release of many captives but ten years later, in 1672, the fund still showed a credit of £4,441. Gardiner's scheme could well have still been contributing since the King, as was his practice with all petitioning royalist officers down on their luck, would have granted a licence for thirteen years.

The market rate clause was a problem since it meant the English slaves were diminishing assets. As Allin reveals, many of them had been sold to poor men, provoking 'several mutinies on the part of their present owners, who were prevented from selling them at a profit.' A greater issue was Charles' inexplicable reluctance to use up the balance of the redemption fund; he argued that the Treaty did not require him to pay up by any specific date and that he himself could not afford to top up the £4,441 at a time when the London merchants were much less generous than before.

Meanwhile, English slaves continued to suffer. One of them was a twenty-year-old apprentice sailor, Sam Daukes, whose ship the *Brothers* was captured by a Turkish man-of-war near Sardinia during a voyage from London to Venice. He was taken to Tunis and then to Algiers where he was sold as a slave and £80 demanded for his ransom, which his family and friends could not pay. In a pitiful but elegantly written letter dated 14 April 1670 and smuggled to his sister, he wrote:

> They made us lie down on our backs, and two men with ropes beat us until the blood ran down our heels; for these three months my diet was bread and vinegar, and that only once a day. They are at me to turn Turk, and to deny my God, which I hope I will not do, even if they kill me. They have threatened, if I do not turn, to beat me on the soles of my feet until the blood runs out of my nose ... if any merchant will advance the money which is for my ransom, I will be his servant, by sea or land, until it is repaid ... the Turks abused the lady and her maid as no Christian would have used a dog, and their backs were blacker than my writing. Had I

been seen writing this letter, I should have received at least 200 blows for it.

It was fortunate for Daukes and the other prisoners, including 140 men from Stepney, that the King finally backed down following an ultimatum from The Dey of Algiers that all English slaves must be redeemed by the end of November 1674.

Despite the way they raised money for such good causes, lotteries were controversial even then. In 1660, the same year that Captain Gardiner made his bid, others were determined to stamp them out. John Croshold, mayor of Norwich, tired of the disruption they caused in the East Anglian city, got together with fifteen other citizens 'to empower the magistrates to limit the stay of the puppet shows and lotteries which injure the trade of the town.' Three years later the King endorsed this stand in a letter which refers to 'the ill consequences resulting from the frequency of lotteries, puppet-shows, etc. whereby the meaner sorts of people are diverted from their work.'

But the unpopularity of lotteries among moralists and others have never deterred successive British Governments in financial difficulties from using them as a source of revenue in addition to taxation. That was why the Whig Government, grappling with a huge national debt on account of Marlborough's wars with the French, launched a national lottery in 1694.

"EITHER WAY, IT'S A LICENCE TO PRINT MONEY"

7

CASHING IN ON SPECULATIVE FEVER
THOMAS NEALE

The time was ripe for another national lottery in the 1690s. Freed from the iron grip of the Puritans, every aspect of life in England had felt the wind of liberation following the restoration of the monarchy in 1660. The financial markets were no exception. In the new permissive, deregulated business era, not unlike the City of London in the 1980s, the stock market boomed.

Investors from dukes to grocers, excited by the prospect of putting to profitable use otherwise redundant capital, poured money into the new-fangled 'joint stock' companies, early ancestors of today's listed companies. Previously, they would have acted like the businessman father of Alexander Pope, who retired from the City to his country seat with a strong-box containing £20,000 in money. That was his 'bank' from which he drew, as necessary, whatever was needed for household expenses. But now you could put your cash in the Insurance Company, Lutespring Company,

Pearl Fishery Company, Glass Bottle Company, Alum Company, Blythe Coal Company, Swordblade Company, Greenland Fishery Company, Tanning Company, Tapestry Company, Copper Company and many others. There was even a Royal Academies Company for educating gentlemen at reasonable rates. In an advertisement the directors announced they had hired scholars and were about to sell 20,000 tickets at 20s. each in a lottery. Two thousand prizes were to be drawn and the winners were to be taught 'Latin, Greek, Hebrew, French, Spanish, conic sections, trigonometry, heraldry, japanning, fortification, book keeping, and the art of playing the theorbo.'

Business was done in busy coffee shops such as Jonathan's or Garraway's near the Royal Exchange and Lloyd's on Lombard Street where brokers, buyers, sellers, proprietors and directors met to argue, bargain and close deals. The three-year boom was stimulated by treasure hunter William Phips returning to London with Spanish gold and other bounty recovered from the wreck of the *Almiranta* which sank off Hispaniola in the West Indies in 1641. News that speculators were paid £5,000 for every £100 they invested in his expedition encouraged fly entrepreneurs to set up a whole raft of similar ventures, in the hope that the public would seize the opportunity to cash in. The Diving Company laid on demonstrations on the banks of the Thames for potential investors who were delighted at the sight of divers, wearing primitive underwater equipment which resembled eccentric suits of armour, plunging into the river and emerging laden with old iron and ship's tackle. Other speculators, banned from investing overseas because of the French wars, put their money into start-up English companies. Paper was a particularly popular choice, as was evident by the regular auctions held by The Company of White Paper-Makers in England at its trading headquarters in Queen Street, London; a typical advertisement announced on 10 October 1693 that it would 'expose by sale by inch of candle several thousand reams of White Writing and Printing Paper.'

Launched into this atmosphere of speculative fever, the 1694 'Million Adventure' lottery, designed to raise £1 million by selling 100,000 tickets for £10 each, was a great success. Tickets were expensive; but, if you could afford them, they were actually as good an investment as speculating in joint stock companies which, as a result, became less popular. The founding of the Bank of England in 1694, with excellent returns on its stock, also helped end this first stock market boom.

The lottery was organised by Thomas Neale, master of the Royal Mint and Groom Porter to Charles II, James II, and William III. He had run a very popular draw the previous year when Richard Haddock, comptroller of the navy, won the top prize of £3,000 and coachmen working for the diarist John Evelyn picked up £40. Ladies and their maids also won prizes; forty per cent of the tickets were bought by women who welcomed a rare opportunity for independent speculation.

Neale has been dismissed as an adventurer who squandered two fortunes and whose duties as Groom Porter, calling the odds when the Palace played at hazard (a game in which two dice were rolled and the resulting numbers bet on), providing playing cards, and settling disputes on the bowling green and gaming table, hardly constituted a serious job. This grossly underestimates him. True, as a gambler and entrepreneur fond of high risk deals, he was irresponsible with money. His reputation was such that when he took over sole control of the Mint in July 1686 the surety asked of him was £15,000 instead of the customary £2,000. His more dubious acquaintances at hazard were the Scottish gambler and duellist John Law, innovative economist to some but crooked banker to others, who later set up France's first national bank and encouraged the insane financial speculation in the Mississippi Bubble which ended in Europe's first stock market crash. Neale was also insolvent when he died in 1699, despite having married England's richest widow known as 'GOLD Neale'. Yet the energetic Groom Porter, whom Sir Isaac Newton succeeded at the Mint, was no lightweight.

Although today he scarcely rates a mention in the history books, he was one of the most effective fixers of the late seventeenth century with contacts everywhere. He was a Member of Parliament for thirty years, a leading light in many of the joint-stock companies, a highly respected coinage expert, and promoter of schemes such as the National Land Bank which pre-dated the Bank of England. His imaginative design for seven radiating streets in the Seven Dials district of London survives and still bears his name.

Neale's career as a lottery entrepreneur began in 1684 following Charles II's irritation over the spivs who flagrantly disregarded the edict that only he could licence lotteries, usually in support of hard-up royalist officers. Repeated press advertisements warning 'Contembers of his Majesties' Letters Patent' to stop selling tickets for unlicensed games were totally ignored. Finally, on 28 July 1684, Charles ordered a clampdown and put Neale in charge. A statement published that day authorised him 'to allow, regulate or suppress all publick Games' and prosecute anyone who disobeyed. Substantial rewards were offered to spies informing on 'the said Rafflings.'

The energetic Groom Porter enthusiastically went about his duties and was able to stem the flood of illegal lotteries. Then, in 1693 and with royal blessing, he launched his own lottery, offering 50,000 tickets at ten shillings each, with 250 prizes of between £5,000 and £20. This was based on a scheme then popular in Venice. Players from aristocrats to domestic servants, who clubbed together to enter, were attracted. They flocked to buy tickets from the London goldsmiths who underwrote the game and set up stalls in coffee shops and taverns such as the Rummer in Whitehall, Three Golden Cocks in Whitehall and Black Horse in the Strand. The draw, which began on 1 November 1693 in the City of London at Freeman's Yard in Cornhill, attracted large crowds; Neale put on a great performance as he officiated over the proceedings, bossing the little Bluecoat boys from Christ's Hospital who drew the tickets. His shouted announcements of the lucky winners were satirised in the burlesque poem *Diluvium Lachrymarum* as:

Rank'd by Groom-Porter Mussulman
The Mufti of this great Divan

The anonymous author was equally as rude about the spectators, 'A jolly crew of gaping Fools' who ranged right across the social spectrum:

Ermine and Vermine, Rags and Scarlets
Promiscuous all, both Lords and Varlets

The lottery itself was mocked as 'From Venice, with a Pox! brought or'e' and the fact that a 'Fortunate Sir Dick!' (Richard Haddock) had won a prize large enough to keep 'Half a score Honest Lads' from starving was highly suspicious.

But the scheme was conducted fairly and properly. Detailed instructions required the goldsmiths and trustees to be witnesses as, prior to the draw, he mixed up the blank and prize tickets in one box, and mixed the numbered tickets in another; both boxes were then sealed and put in a huge chest with five strong locks with keys guarded by five of the witnesses. The Treasury, despite objecting he was a dodgy gambler, eventually decided that the Groom Porter was the man best qualified to oversee the national 1694 draw.

Neale decided there should be 2,500 prizes. Top prize was £1,000 a year (won by Monsieur Cock, a French refugee and politician), with nine at £500 and twenty at £100, all payable for sixteen years. In addition, ticket holders who did not win prizes were held to have given a £10 loan to the government by their purchase of a ticket and were thus entitled to a fixed rate of interest of £1 per year over the sixteen-year period. What the Government was doing was borrowing money from the public to supply its growing need for credit and using lotteries to make the terms more attractive. It was, however, slow to pay up and winners, who held a number of public protest meetings, eventually had to petition Parliament to get what they were owed.

The lottery encouraged hundreds of unofficial draws, mainly in London but also in the provinces. Prizes ranged from a dancing school in York to new law books, entire libraries and fancy hats. They became too many for Neale to regulate effectively, and his moral position was undermined both by his own private lotteries, even though these were perfectly legal, and by his dabbling in the more dubious joint-stock companies.

In 1695, an acerbic broadside against banks, lotteries and joint-stock companies for allegedly destroying trade was launched in a pamphlet entitled *Angliae Tutamen, or The Safety of England*. It thundered:

> What a Run of Lotteries have we had! That like a Plague have spread themselves over the whole Kingdom ... every Body is sick of them.

Samuel Pepys certainly was. He complained to Isaac Newton that lotteries had extinguished all conversation save debate on the chances of winning. Yet they continued to be marketed through handbills in coffee shops and inns and newspaper advertisements under such names as *The Golden Chance, Treble Chance*, and *The Fair Adventure*, reminiscent of titles like *The Mint* and *Big Game TV* of the interactive television quiz shows investigated in 2006 as disguised lotteries.

Women jumped on the bandwagon with a lottery called *The Ladies' Invention*. It claimed sixpence could win £1,000 and eighteen pence £2,000, 'without disadvantages of Blanks as in other lotteries.' The publicity added:

> This being an Invention of the Female Sex, we hear several Ladies of quality design to venture considerable sums in it. Tickets may be had in most coffee Houses in town.

The female entrepreneurs also seemed to be as anxious as the ancient Greeks to show the draw was above board; *The Flying Post* of 15 November 1698 assured readers that the wheel to be used 'will be after a new mode with 24 Glass Squares, that the Billets therein will be visible to every Spectator.' This was displayed for inspection at Frank's Coffee House near the Royal Exchange, where the draw, after repeated delays, was eventually held on 25 March 1699.

Rancorous spats between competing lottery operators were common. A game called *The Wheel of Fortune* planned elaborate entertainment during its 1698 draw at the Theatre Royal in Dorset Gardens. It promised:

> During a symphony of music the curtain rises very slowly and discovers two wheels upon the stage; then two Figures, representing Fortune and Astraea, the Goddess of Justice descend over each wheel, in two rich Chariots gilt with gold.

This annoyed the organiser of *The Hopeful Adventurer* game; he had chosen as a venue the less dramatic Music Room at York Buildings, where the draw was postponed so often that people demanded their money back. In the public prints he claimed 'some villains' (his rivals at *The Wheel of Fortune*) had given the impression that his lottery had already been drawn. Within days, underwriters at *The Wheel of Fortune* hit back at 'this false report' that they were misleading the market. As evidence that their own draw was trustworthy, they printed the names of recent top prize winners who included a barrister, a minister of religion, the wife of a London merchant, and a footman.

Contemporary dramatists were quick to satirize the game; one play, *The Fool's Expectation* was acted at the Theatre Royal, the very spot where the real-life draw had been held. They were also satirized in a remarkable tract, *The Arraignment, Trial and Condemnation of Squire Lottery, alias Royal Oak Lottery, London, 1699.* The numerous frauds cited in this mock trial were alleged to be true: a peer's steward lost an estate of his own worth £300 a year and £4,000 of his master's money; a west India widow lost, in less than a month, the cargo of two ships, valued at £1,500.

So many people were being swindled all over the country that, as the French had done thirty-eight years earlier, Parliament outlawed private lotteries. The 1699 legislation said 'evil-disposed persons' had set up 'many mischievous and unlawful games' and had thereby 'most unjustly and fraudulently got to themselves great sums of money from the children and servants of several gentlemen, traders and merchants, and from other unwary persons, to the utter ruin and impoverishment of many families.' The demise of these 'Prodigious Follies' was celebrated in a poem of 1700 which accorded Neale, who had died the year before, the just Epitaph:

Under this Stone does the Groom-Porter lie
Who Liv'd by Chance, and Dy'd by Destiny,
Whene'er Good Soul from Mortal Body flies
Earth takes the Blanks, and Heaven receives the Prize.

The ban on all lotteries, unless authorised by the state, was to last 235 years until 1934 when it was partially lifted by the Betting and Lotteries Act.

SO JOHN ISN'T THE ONLY BLUNT
WITH A 'CRIMINAL' RECORD!

8

CASHING IN ON
SPECULATIVE FEVER
JOHN BLUNT

The success of the 1694 lottery encouraged the career of one of the greatest chancers in history: conman John Blunt, brash, energetic, and a shrewd psychologist of enormous charm. Over a remarkably long period he was able to exploit brilliantly the greed and credibility of his victims. From the start this rich self-made man had an eye to the main chance; one of his early fortunes came from underwriting a linen manufacturer at a time when one in five London workers were employed in the textile and clothing industry. A creature of the era of scams and dodgy business schemes, indeed its very essence writ large, Blunt finally achieved his ambition of getting closer to the centre of political power.

An opportunity to enrich himself further came in 1710 when the Tories finally ousted the Whigs. The new chancellor of the Exchequer, Robert Harley, had inherited a huge national debt but could not find the money to pay it off; the Whig-dominated Bank of England and East India Company were reluctant to lend any, and further taxation was not an option given the large amounts already raised for Marlborough's armies.

Help was at hand. Blunt persuaded Harley that the answer was a new state lottery organized on a scale never before attempted. The 1710 lottery providing thirty-two-year annuities from 14s. per annum for blank tickets to up to £1,000 per annum for prize-winning tickets had not raised the hoped-for gross revenues of £1.5 million. It had not caught the public's imagination, though all classes seemed to have supported it; 'som very ordinary creature has gott 400 pounds a year,' complained Lady Wentworth in a letter to her son.

With a great fanfare, the new game, also designed to raise £1.5 million, was launched on Tuesday 13 March 1711. Prize money totalled nearly £700,000, a huge amount for the time, with the top prize being set at £12,000. There were 24,999 other prizes of varying amounts down to £20. The fledgling Bank of England, then starting to find its feet and establish its authority, again became the receiver of public money for the state lottery.

As was the case with the 1694 lottery, the punters, mostly well-off merchants living in the Square Mile, could not lose, save for some capital depreciation on their investment. They not only received six per cent interest on their £10 ticket but a five to one chance of a prize, compared to a thirty-nine to one chance the previous year. People queued to play at coffee shops and taverns all over the City of London. They ranged from the essayist and co-founder of *The Spectator*, Joseph Addison, who won a £1,000 prize, down to footmen. Stockbrokers, who handled the lottery tickets as a sideline to share dealing, sold all 150,000 tickets within hours and turned away many disappointed investors. 'It was impossible to do it though I was very early,' wrote one. *The Post Boy* reported:

> There was such a Crowd of People, and Merchants have received such Commissions from Abroad that 'tis not to be doubted that double that sum would have been subscribed that very day.

Shortly after, Blunt launched a second lottery called *The Adventure of Two Millions, or The Classis*, designed to raise £2 million and mainly aimed at the seriously rich. The 20,000 tickets, which were all again quickly snapped up, cost £100 each or went for lesser amounts if the stockbrokers sold shares in them. This made it easier for the emerging professional classes, such as surgeons, apothecaries, scriveners, clergymen even, to take part in addition to the usual aristocrats, merchants and wealthy aldermen.

Cleverly, Blunt borrowed a scheme pioneered in earlier Continental lotteries, which used so-called 'Class' draws, with prizes graduated into First, Second and Third sections. Nothing if not innovative, he went further and divided the draw into five classes. First Class (or Classis) offered 1,330 tickets with prizes from £110 to £1,000; Second Class, 2,670 tickets with prizes from £115 to £3,000; Third Class, 4,000 prizes from £120 to £4,000; and Fourth Class, 5,340 tickets from £125 to £5,000. A fifth and final draw of 6,660 tickets, with prizes from £130 to a top prize of £20,000 (won by London merchant Thomas Weddell), was held as a great climax to the game.

Some investors, such as the duchess of Newcastle, who held eleven winning tickets and the dukes of Rutland and Buckingham, who held eight each, did extremely well. Harley himself was not so lucky. Just five days before the announcement of his first lottery scheme he was nearly stabbed to death by a French spy, the Marquis de Guiscard, whom he and other privy councillors were interrogating. Suddenly the treacherous nobleman, suspected of plotting to assassinate Queen Anne, drew a knife and struck Harley twice with such force that the blade broke against his rib, causing the Council 'to rise and draw their swords in their defence, as if a wild Beast had been let loose among them.'

Predictably, the two lotteries did the job. Harley, despite being on his sickbed for six weeks, was delighted with the £3.5 million raised for the Exchequer coffers, and was rewarded with a peerage. The official citation for his becoming earl of Oxford explained how he 'prevented the further Plundering of the Nation, and also provided for the Settling of a New Trade to the South Seas and by rescuing Public Credit so opportunely Relieved the Languishing Condition of the Treasury.' Unfortunately, this ultimately proved to be a financial smoke and mirrors illusion; the government had to continue to pay interest on each lottery ticket sold, which were effectively loans whose holders could redeem them at will. It is likely that the superficially bright idea of consolidating debt not secured against revenues to be realized from taxation eventually cost the Government around £9 million.

There is a theory that, by raising the stakes with large prize money, Blunt's lottery also laid the foundation for the setting up, announced by Harley on 2 May 1711, of the doomed speculative venture, the South Sea Company.

Harley intended this trading company, which Blunt put together with London merchant George Caswall, to become a new financial institution to rival the Bank of England and the East India Company. The idea was that it would boost trade in the South Seas and take over a part of the national debt, converting it into shares in the new company. That meant investors holding government debt from which they received guaranteed interest payments from the Treasury had to be persuaded to swap the money they were owed for an equity stake in a company with absolutely no business track record. Blunt was well up to this task. They believed his assurances that the share price would keep rising on account of the untold riches to be discovered in South America. It was a classic example of the El Dorado syndrome that only a century before had persuaded prospective immigrants that the newly established colony of Virginia in the wilds of North America was a veritable Garden of Eden.

It spawned all kinds of nonsense, from companies promising sunshine from cucumbers, a wheel for perpetual motion, mobile office buildings, to that enduring classic, 'an undertaking of Great Advantage but no-one to know what it is.'

The South Sea Company, initiating a tradition that continues today in spectacular company collapses from Rolls Royce to

Northern Rock, was built on sand. It never was a proper trading company, its wealth was entirely on paper and scarcely any investors questioned whether it had ever made a profit. Sleight of hand and market manipulation by Blunt and his fellow crooks kept it afloat until the inevitable spectacular crash of 1720. This financially ruined many aristocrats, MPs, peers and even a genius like Isaac Newton, who sadly forgot share prices cannot defy the laws of financial gravity. 'I can calculate the motions of heavenly bodies but not the madness of people,' he said.

Tulipmania, gold rushes, fine art speculation, the dotcom bubble, dodgy mortgages bubble and the hedge fund boom are all manifestations of the 'irrational exuberance' which has periodically gripped greedy investors down the ages. The urge to believe the impossible, encouraged by the uber cunning Blunts, Maxwells and Savundras of this world, plausible shamen of financial dreams, will always trigger off market madness. It is this that fuelled the speculative frenzy culminating in the South Sea Company disaster. Lotteries were the symptom, not the root cause.

"I CAN SEE THAT YOUR
LUCKY NUMBERS ARE
34-22-36..."

9

LOVER OF MONEY

CASANOVA

Giacomo Casanova was far more than one of the world's most energetic lovers. This notorious Venetian polymath was a diplomat, a soldier, a spy, a black magician, a friar, a scientist, a lawyer, a mathematician, an astronomer, a financier, a gambler – and a very effective organizer of lotteries. With its unpredictability and reliance on the mysterious workings of fate and chance, the game has always attracted unusual personalities, but none so eccentric as Casanova, whose exploits all over Europe, both in and out of bed, have made his name a legend.

One of his greatest achievements in the financial field was to help found the French state lottery. It made him, briefly, a millionaire, and it eventually became such a well-loved national institution that even the fall of the Bastille in 1789, and guillotining of Louis XVI and Marie Antoinette in 1793, did not cause it to miss a single draw. Later, Casanova toured Europe intending to set up similar schemes in London, Berlin, Warsaw and Moscow, but he never managed to repeat his French success story.

Casanova, aged thirty-two, arrived in Paris on 5 January 1757 after a spectacular escape from the most secure prison in Europe, 'The Steps', attached to the Doge's Palace in Venice, where the Inquisition had incarcerated him on suspicion of experimenting in alchemy. His night flight across treacherous rooftops turned him into a celebrity in Parisian society; everybody wanted to hear his dramatic tale. This made it easier to insinuate himself into circles where he could exploit his charm and guile to make the money that he desperately needed to survive. In this mission, he was greatly aided by a very influential contact he had met during sexual adventures at a private casino on Murano Island off Venice three years previously: the Abbe Francois Joachim de Pierre de Bernis, recently promoted to foreign minister of France. When they first met in 1753, de Bernis, an aristocrat who trained for the Church but changed to diplomacy, was French Ambassador to the Republic of Venice and lover of a tall, beautiful nun M.M., whose identity has never been confirmed but who also happened to be one of Casanova's many mistresses. De Bernis, who was addicted to watching couples, threesomes, and foursomes, owned the casino where he had installed luxurious bedrooms decorated with pornographic paintings and devices that allowed the beds to be viewed secretly from adjoining rooms. Casanova, who was very proud of his sexual prowess, had no problem in letting de Bernis spy on his energetic all-night orgies with M.M., who used to complain after that he was so vigorous her hips ached. Ever considerate for the needs of their onlooker, he would place cushions under the nun's bottom and make her raise each leg in turn so that the ogling ambassador had a better view of her vagina.

When they met at Versailles, de Bernis showed his gratitude to Casanova for indulging his voyeurism by readily agreeing to do him a favour; he suggested introducing him, as an outstanding financial expert, to King Louis XV's octogenarian comptroller-general Jean de Boulogne, who headed the Department of Finance. But before this meeting took place, he advised the Venetian adventurer that he should think up a project profitable to the French Exchequer, nothing too complicated or chimerical, a project that increased revenues without raising taxes. This completely stumped Casanova. As he confesses in his *Memoirs of My Life*:

> Having not the faintest notion of finances, no matter how I racked my brains all the ideas that came to me were only for new taxes and since they all struck me as odious or absurd, I rejected them all.

Undeterred by the knowledge that he had no idea what to suggest, Casanova went ahead and met the finance minister, who told him 20 million francs were urgently needed to finance the *Ecole Militaire*, the king's military cadet school founded by his mistress, Madame de Pompadour. For Louis XV to provide the money from the royal treasury was just not politically possible; for the same reason, a bail-out from state taxes was also out of the question. Monsieur de Boulogne had brought with him Monsieur Joseph de Paris-Duverney, superintendent of the school since 1751 and a famous financier. They asked Casanova directly for his ideas. Bluffing hard, Casanova said:

> 'I have a plan in mind which would yield the King the return on a hundred million (francs).'
> Duverney: 'How much would such a yield cost the King?'
> Casanova: 'Only the expense of collecting it.'
> Duverney: 'Then it is the nation which would supply the revenue?'
> Casanova: 'Yes, but voluntarily.'

Wisely, Casanova did not elaborate but, to his surprise, Duverney said he knew what the scheme was. It was one that had been tried before and there were insurmountable difficulties. However, he was prepared to discuss it further over lunch the following day.

The next morning Casanova was in low spirits when he took a hackney coach along frozen roads to Duverney's beautiful chateau at Neuilly-Plaisance, to the east of Paris. He was well aware that he could not fool the man who, forty years earlier, had saved the French economy from hyper-inflation following crashes caused by another chancer John Law, the Scottish gambler who had, bizarrely, been put in charge of France's finances. So it was with uncharacteristic nervousness that Casanova joined the lunch party. Warming themselves before a huge fire were eight men, including three or four officials from the French treasury. Casanova was introduced as a friend of both the foreign affairs minister and comptroller-general. He did not take part in the chit-chat about wars, scandals and the freezing of the Seine, as he had decided on a strategy of staying silent for as long as possible. After ninety minutes at the table, Duverney took Casanova to his study with another guest, a fellow Italian, a diplomat aged about fifty called Giovanni Calzabigi. Two officials joined them. With a smile, the minister produced a folio notebook and said: 'There is your plan.'

Casanova studied the title page. Without hesitation, he handed it back and agreed, with huge relief, 'That is my plan.' It was a scheme for a state lottery. Duverney, clearly enjoying himself, then told him he had been forestalled; the idea was Calzabigi's. This left Casanova, who was nothing if not quick on the uptake, totally unfazed. He replied with words to the effect that great minds think alike and swiftly moved the discussion on to the issue of why it had not been implemented.

The lottery was simple enough in concept. Each month five numbers were drawn at random from a total of ninety. Players could bet on a single number, an *extrait* (for a prize 15 times the stake), or on a combination of two numbers, an *ambe* (a prize 270 times the stake), three numbers, a *terne* (a prize 4,800 times the stake), or four numbers, a *quaterne* (60,000 times the stake). If they hit the jackpot by getting all five numbers, a *quine*, in the same drawing, their prize was worth a million times the stake.

This system dated back to the method of election of the five-man council that ruled the city state of Genoa in the sixteenth and seventeenth centuries; ninety names of eligible candidates were written on slips and placed in an urn, from which five were drawn. Citizens began betting on who would be selected with such enthusiasm that the authorities adapted the system for a financial lottery with ninety numbers, which was officially instituted in 1620. From that time onwards it became the model for many of the early state lotteries set up throughout Italy, and later, other parts of Europe.

The 'insurmountable' difficulty that so concerned Duverney was not a moral one. Louis XV was content for his subjects to gamble; the problem was whether they would gamble in sufficient numbers to ensure the lottery made a profit. Theoretically it was possible for the King to be unlucky in a number of early draws if, say, a player got a *quine*, paying out a million to one. The odds against this were, however, astronomical: 1 in 44 million, nearly three times the odds in the UK National Lottery. Even the odds of winning a *quaterne*, paying out 60,000 to one, were immense at 1 in 500,000. Over the long run, provided sufficient revenue was raised, the King was bound to win under the scheme proposed. Yet the risk-adverse royal advisers, temperamentally conservative in financial matters, remained unconvinced and feared heavy losses for which they would be blamed.

Duverney pressed Casanova hard:

Will you not admit that at the very first drawing the King can lose an immense sum?

Casanova replied:

Between possibility and reality there is infinity; but I admit it. If the King loses a great sum at the first drawing, the success of the lottery is assured. Moral forces are calculated like probabilities. You know that all insurance companies are rich. I will prove to you before all the mathematicians in Europe that, granted God is neutral, it is impossible that the King will not make a profit of one in five by this lottery.

He argued that if the people believed Louis XV was prepared to lose, say, 100 million francs, this would dazzle them and guarantee substantial sales over a sufficiently long period for him to make a profit (thus saving the *Ecole Militaire* from insolvency).

The elderly minister, more willing to innovate than his younger colleagues despite having to mop up after Law, was convinced by the projected profit of twenty per cent overall and invited Casanova, now confidently creating business plans off the top of his head, to persuade the council of ministers and senior treasury officials responsible for the royal school. Meanwhile Calzabigi, impressed by his fellow countryman's spin-doctoring and certain their lottery plans were identical, suggested they joined forces to push the project through. His elder brother, the financier Ranier Calzabigi, who had devised the plan, would work out the mathematical details while Casanova sold the idea to sceptics.

At a three-hour session of the school council, which the famous mathematician Jean Le Rond d'Alembert attended as expert witness, the trio of Italians put their case and answered all objections. Casanova, who took the lead, again relied heavily on his analogy with insurance companies (then starting to expand from covering only marine risks) who spread risks over a period to make a profit overall. According to his memoirs he ended the marathon presentation by saying:

> There was not a man at once learned and honourable in the world who could offer to be at the head of this lottery on the understanding that it would win at every drawing, and that if a man should appear with the temerity to give them that assurance they should turn him out, because either he would not keep his promise or, if he kept it, he would be a scoundrel.

The wily Duverney clinched the case by pointing out that they could always abolish the lottery if it failed.

The plan was approved with the financial backing of Louis and a decree issued appointing Jean Calzabigi as administrator and

Casanova as director, for which he received a basic salary of 4,000 francs a year (about £11,200) and six lottery offices. He promptly sold five and set up the sixth in luxurious quarters in fashionable Rue Saint-Denis with his valet, a sharp Italian who had worked in the diplomatic service, as chief clerk. Bonuses linked to a fixed percentage of the profits boosted his income to at least 120,000 francs a year (about £336,000), allowing him to swank round Paris in a carriage and receive unlimited credit. His wealth was not, however, a done deal; the lottery had to work first. This was not guaranteed initially.

For Casanova, the first drawing on 18 April 1758 was highly profitable since his promise to pay all winning tickets within twenty-four hours instead of the customary seven days ensured 'everyone came to my office for tickets', prompting angry complaints from fifty clerks working at the other offices. Duverney complained he had made too much. On the second drawing, however, sales fell and a *terne* of 40,000 francs (about £120,000) forced him to borrow money. After initial setbacks, the monthly lottery went on to become a huge success, establishing Casanova's reputation as a financier and making him a popular figure. From September 1758 to the end of 1759 he is listed as a director of the venture. Everywhere he went, salons, theatre lobbies and even the street, he was mobbed for the tickets he always carried with him, so that he always returned home with 'pockets full of money.'

The military school, in whose cause the scheme had been set up also prospered. Eight years later the French Treasury, anxious to increase state revenues, hijacked the lottery with the agreement of the new king, Louis XVI, and turned it into the famous 'Loterie Royale de France', employing 20,000 people. It thrived until November 1793 when, under the rule of the revolutionary Terror, it was abolished following a petition from the Commune of Paris which insisted: 'this immoral institution must not exist under a republican regime. Only kings lay traps for those they rule.'

Barely four years later, it was reinstated by popular demand; even the leaders of the revolution could not resist the French public's love of a flutter. Thereafter, the lottery ran continuously until May 1836, and then, in common with most other European state lotteries, it was dropped because of moral objections and declining sales. At its height in 1811, the net proceeds amounted to four per cent of the national budget, and there were three draws a month not only in Paris but Lyon, Strasbourg, Bordeaux and Brussels, all run with typical Gallic efficiency. It became an integral part of French culture. Napoleon Bonaparte personally ordered subsidiaries to be set up in the territories he conquered, including Turin, Genoa, Florence, Hamburg and also Rome, where it replaced the Papal lottery. In 1816, a *Times* correspondent compared its British counterpart unfavourably, complaining that draws were held 'six or seven times a year only in London, whereas in France they are three or four times a month everywhere, in Paris and four other cities.'

As he suspected it would, given his intuitive understanding of the lure of betting, Casanova's legacy lasted. Although his memoirs do not state it explicitly, he tried to replicate it in England where, with some exceptions, lotteries were mainly inducements to investors to buy new issues of government loans in the form of annuities. This was why he went to London in June 1763, braving a rough Channel crossing on a packet shared with the duke of Bedford, English ambassador to France. Circumstantial evidence such as his dealings with London insurance offices suggests he hoped to use his key contacts to win a licence for a state draw run on the French model. Rich aristocrats such as the duke of Cumberland, duchess of Northumberland, duchess of Grafton and Augustus Hervey, Lord Bristol, already regularly invested already in the old-style schemes; they could expect to make much more money, either as players or operators, in a more exciting, chance-orientated game. Unfortunately, Casanova never saw his most influential patron Charles Wyndham, Lord Egremont, a Government Minister and one of the nation's most wealthy peers, who died suddenly on 21 August 1763 shortly after Casanova's arrival in England, of a stroke caused by overeating. Another celebrated figure whom he knew well and who could have helped was his former mistress, Mme Cornelys, who rented Carlisle House in Soho Square for her glittering risqué salons, but they fell out. He was introduced at court to King George III and Queen Charlotte, though there is no record that this royal endorsement aided his business ambitions. Casanova, now styling himself the Chevalier de Seingalt, spent nine months in England. He pursued women, including the notorious courtesan La Charpillon (later John Wilkes' mistress), gambled and possibly spied until suddenly he had to flee for his life from London for having stood surety for a forged bill of exchange.

For the next three and a half years Casanova roamed all over Europe and Russia, intermittently pursuing his dreams of setting up another lottery. In Berlin, where a lottery was first set up in 1740, Jean Calzabigi had been running a scheme for Frederick the Great for two years, but the King had withdrawn the State's financial backing and insisted Calzabigi continue it at his own risk. Casanova drew up a rescue plan and tried, unsuccessfully, to persuade Calzabigi, who was spending money like a madman and drowning in debt, to go into partnership with him again. Eventually, he managed to arrange a meeting with Frederick in the Sans Souci Gardens, where they talked about the lottery, but did not get on; the King described it as 'an elaborate swindle'; Casanova complained the Prussian monarch eyed him as he would a handsome footman.

He failed again in St Petersburg with Catherine the Great who turned him down on the grounds that implementing a lottery in the vast country of Russia was impractical. There was also no luck in Warsaw where King Stanislaus II of Poland, one of hundreds of Catherine's former lovers, was put off by the many rumours he had heard about his exotic visitor. Casanova ended his days working in humiliating conditions as a librarian in a castle in Bohemia where he was absorbed in writing, almost non-stop, the twenty-five volumes of his remarkable memoirs. He still had time for a pet project: teasing out a system for winning the Rome lottery. But death intervened before he could complete it.

"NOW THAT'S WHAT I CALL
HIGHWAY ROBBERY!"

10

FLEECING THE PUBLIC
CHARLES 'PATCH' PRICE

The lottery has traditionally been a licence for fraudsters and conmen to print money. One of the most notorious tricksters was an eighteenth-century psychopath called Charles 'Patch' Price, who managed to support a wife and eight children at boarding school through his fiddles. Some criminals seem pre-programmed to be totally amoral, lacking all sense of right and wrong. They are, thankfully, very rare, but unmistakable when they emerge. Charles Price, though entirely forgotten today, was one of them.

By the age of twelve he had developed such a talent for fraud and deceit that his father, a respectable tailor who, in the early 1700s, had brought his family from south Wales to Monmouth Street, then London's second-hand clothes centre, disinherited him in despair.

From an early age he used his great acting skill to defraud practically everyone who crossed his path, making the equivalent of £5 million today. Extensive travelling on a tour of Europe as a gentleman's servant gave him a plausible sophistication, which disguised his criminality. He swindled a hatter to whom he was apprenticed, defrauded the revenue when he was a brewer, tricked a business partner out of £6,000 (£300,000 in today's money), and took a Mrs Pouteney as mistress, but eloped with her niece. For Price, becoming a lottery office keeper must have seemed like Christmas every day.

He moved from the insalubrious Seven Dials district of London, a higgledy-piggledy Irish ghetto of narrow streets and ramshackle tenement buildings – it had degenerated dramatically since the founder Neale's day – to the much more genteel Knightsbridge, where he passed himself off as a stockbroker. This was not unusual as many stockbrokers doubled up as lottery office keepers. He won the confidence of a retired grocer even persuading him to take banknotes into the City of London to be changed into smaller ones. Then he pulled off an ingenious sting, an early variant of the Nigerian email scam. He conned his new acquaintance into believing he was a close friend of a Mr Bond (whose very name should have aroused suspicion), a very old and very rich retired broker whose only living relative was a fifty-year-old sister who was determined to remain single. Price's story was that the old gentleman had not only asked him to be his executor but to find a second, equally trustworthy, executor.

Price told his victim:

Here is an opportunity for us to make a considerable sum in a short time, and, in all probability, a very capital fortune in a few years; for, the sister being determined not to marry, and having no relatives in the world, there is no doubt but she will leave us the whole of the estate; and, after his decease, she will become totally dependent upon us. I shall see the old gentleman, Mr Bond, today, and, if you will join in the trust, the will shall be immediately made.

Foolishly, the ex-grocer agreed. Next day at noon he visited 'Mr Bond' at a house in Leather Lane where the sister (Price's accomplice

Mrs Pouteney) showed him in and introduced him to her brother, who was lying wearily across two chairs with a night cap wrapped round his head. In a convincingly quavering voice, interrupted by throaty coughs, Mr Bond (Price in disguise, of course) apologised for the absence of his old – and most untrustworthy – friend, Mr Price who, unfortunately, had needed to leave for a business appointment at a City coffee house, but would meet him there at 1pm.

When they met there, Price suggested they visit Mr Bond together but, on calling on him, they were told by the sister that her brother had just left for a coach outing to Highgate Hill. And so the charade continued for several days until, eventually, the will was drawn up and, on the strength of his becoming an executor and the huge fortune this would eventually yield, the grocer was defrauded by Price out of £1,000 in cash (£50,000 today) and bonds totalling £200.

As a lottery office keeper, Price was up to every scam going, cheerfully conning his customers through selling dud tickets and then fleeing from them when they discovered how they had been tricked. Like an early Arthur Daly, he constantly had to keep moving offices to keep one step ahead of the outraged mob whose revenge was to demolish the premises. His last office was at the corner of King Street in Covent Garden where he was in partnership with two other rogues, Matthew Oliver and Jacob Franks. He was driven out in 1780.

He then began a career as a forger by counterfeiting Bank of England notes to such an astonishingly high standard that the engraving, signature and watermarks were virtually indistinguishable from the genuine article. As the forged notes flooded on to the market, the bank directors came close to panic as they failed repeatedly to detect the source. With the execution in July 1779 of William Matthewson, an expert banknote forger who could reproduce watermarks 'which the maker thought impossible to be done', they thought the forgery issue was settled. For them, the problem was serious. Confidence in the bank's paper money was essential to its growing reputation as a sound commercial organization managing seventy per cent of the national debt. 'The stability of the Bank of England is equal to that of the British Government', declared the economist Adam Smith just four years earlier in his 1776 free trade treatise, *The Wealth of Nations*.

Price was more successful than Matthewson because he was a one-man band. Save for his mistress, he had no accomplices to grass him up. He engraved his own plates, made his own ink to forge signatures, manufactured his own paper with the watermark and, suitably disguised, introduced the notes himself. Even his wife had no idea of his chicanery.

The bank printed advertisements in newspapers, on wall posters, and printed handbills delivered house to house in central London, which minutely described his various disguises:

> [He] has worn a black patch over his left eye, tied with a string round his head, sometimes wears a white wig ... walks with a short crutch stick with an ivory head, stoops or affects to stoop very much and walks slow as if infirm.

For some months he stopped, during which time the bank obtained a legal decision that it was not liable to pay forged notes, but then he resumed forging and circulating banknotes with impunity for an amazing six years through a series of typically devious schemes.

Through a newspaper advertisement he hired, at a weekly salary of 18s., a male servant called Samuel to look after, at 39 Tichfield Street near Oxford Circus, a young nobleman allegedly then in Bedfordshire. Prior to his arrival, Samuel was to be servant to an old man called Brank (Price in disguise again).

After a few days Brank, explaining the nobleman wished to buy lottery tickets, gave Samuel a forged £20 and a forged £40 note and told him to buy them at offices in the Haymarket and Charing Cross. Innocently, Samuel did so and, having passed this test, was entrusted with forged notes of a much larger value – up to £400 – with which to buy tickets at other lottery offices such as Goodluck's, clustered round the Royal Exchange in the City. This was a convenient way of laundering money.

The guinea he received for this service scarcely compensated for his subsequent arrest and imprisonment in Bridewell prison. Fortunately for him, the Bow Street runners believed his story, and Samuel agreed to co-operate in catching Price. A trap was sprung but failed to ensnare him on account of real stupidity on the part of the authorities.

They decided to pounce after Brank sent Samuel a message to meet him the following day in Mill's Coffee House at 11pm precisely. The runners told him to go, but to be five minutes late so they could stake out the scene. As a tactic this was inept, since Price was cunning and cautious, arriving punctually and taking the precaution of arriving in a coach from where he could check out, unobserved, what was happening. And what he saw was Samuel talking to a disguised runner just up the street from Mill's. He fled immediately; the subsequent police raid on the Tichfield Street house was pointless since Price had hired it for one week only and had long left. He went on laundering false notes of above £40 (£20 and £40 notes having become too suspect) and even hiring another young manservant to introduce them into the system. On at least one more occasion the runners missed this English Scarlet Pimpernel by minutes.

Eventually, his luck ran out. He was caught, with banknotes worth £300 in his pockets, and questioned at Bow Street, but securing a conviction did not prove easy since Samuel, who could identify him only by his voice, had never seen him except in disguise. Arrogant and insolent to the end, Price had one more trick to pull, which almost worked.

Imprisoned in Bridewell prison, he sent for his wife and eldest son who until then were unaware that he was a master criminal, and told them everything. Then he wrote a letter to Mrs Pouteney, telling her to burn all his disguises, to dismantle and destroy his elaborate forging equipment and to melt down his engraved plates. He concealed the letter in the sole of his son's boot, and it was smuggled out of Bridewell and delivered to Mrs Pouteney, who diligently carried out his instructions, giving the boy the charred pieces of plate to bury in some nearby fields.

Unfortunately for Price, the plates were discovered and used as evidence against him. Even at this stage he kept his cool and succeeded, by yet another ruse, to avoid the humiliation of a public execution. It is, however, a considerable mystery why, given his proven escapologist skills, he did not try and follow the example of those folk heroes who freed themselves from Newgate and other prisons, to popular acclaim. Take Jack Sheppard, who inspired the character of Captain Macheath in John Gay's *The Beggar's Opera* and was more well-known among the poor than the monarchy. He escaped no fewer than six times, often disguised as a beggar, butcher or even, in *Toad of Toad Hall* mode, as a washerwoman.

Like Jack, who as a former carpenter's apprentice knew how to use a wide variety of tools, Price possessed the technical expertise to escape from confinement and restraints. Proof positive of this was his ability to forge bank notes with such precision. Why he did not try is truly surprising; perhaps he had simply given up. Instead, he used his cunning to stage an ingenious suicide. And, unlike the celebrated thief-taker Jonathan Wild, who tried unsuccessfully to poison himself to cheat the gallows, Price succeeded. He told his long-suffering son that he wished to write a private letter, but feared the warders would catch sight of it by suddenly bursting into his room, as was their habit. To prevent this, he gave him money to buy two gimlets and a cord so that he could screw the gimlets to the frame of the door and fasten the cord across the door which opened inwards.

What he actually did was to fasten the gimlets under two hat screws – and hang himself, on 24 January 1786, just ten days after his commitment for a forgery on the Bank of England. So died, according to *The Times*, 'the greatest swindler, or professed Cheat, that ever inhabited Great Britain.'

As was customary with suicides, he was buried at crossroads near Bridewell with a stake driven through his heart. But, a week later, the body was removed by night, probably by the faithful Mrs Pouteney who, though cross-examined brutally and at length, did not incriminate her former lover. She had evidently forgiven him for his fling with her niece.

II

FOUNDING THE BRITISH MUSEUM

SWINDLER PETER LEHEUP

London 1753

The cosmopolitan English capital was at the height of its fame and influence – financial centre of the world, great hive of culture, richest and largest city in Europe. Small wonder that this was where the world's first national museum was founded, open to everyone and which today, still free of charge, attracts nearly five million visitors every year. More than £45 million of lottery money helped finance its latest innovation, the £110 million glass-roofed Great Court, designed by Norman Foster, which has unified so imaginatively the British Museum's disparate mid-nineteenth-century galleries since 2000. But the bad-tempered public spat about the stone used in the reconstructed south portico was nothing compared to the row over the dishonestly conducted lottery which set up the museum itself in 1753.

The chance came with a bequest from Sir Hans Sloane, physician to the famous and promoter of milk chocolate, to leave his huge collection of books and other treasures, worth about £100,000, to the nation in exchange for a dowry of £20,000 for his two daughters. Under the terms of his will, if this offer was not taken up within twelve months of his death then the collection, 70,000 objects in all, would be offered to a European Academy of Sciences, and thus lost to the nation. Unfortunately, no money was available.

King George II, philistine as ever, dismissed the idea of public funding with a curt: 'I don't think there are twenty thousand pounds in the Treasury.' Members of Parliament were also not initially interested until the Commons Speaker, Arthur Onslow, successfully lobbied for the idea of buying the collection with the proceeds of a public lottery. His greatest challenge was the chancellor of the Exchequer, Henry Pelham, who opposed lotteries on principle and could only be won round with an agreement that the act of Parliament authorising the draw would set out elaborate rules to prevent fraud and heavy penalties for violation.

Regrettably the trustees, who included the archbishop of Canterbury, the Lord Chancellor and the Speaker of the House of Commons, chose as one of the chief organizers a man who cheerfully broke every rule, provoking a mighty public scandal, an acrimonious Commons debate and the intervention of the King. He was Peter Leheup, a corrupt stock jobber. Appointing him was about as sensible as trusting Dracula to look after a blood bank. Leheup was a noted crook and 'odious character' famous for financial chicanery in Hanover, and whose very name was synonymous with swindling (in the same way that centuries later 'conradisation', after the disgraced media mogul Conrad Black, became a term for financial misconduct in some City circles). Even in 1739 the politician Bolingbroke could write to his friend Marchmont: 'Walpole is your tyrant today; and any man His Majesty pleases to name – Horace or Leheup – may be so tomorrow.'

With four other crooked stock jobbers, Leheup set about systematically circumventing the lottery legislation which received the royal assent on 7 June 1753, even sending a circular to his accomplices, one of whom later fled to France, setting out precisely how to rig the market.

Chancellor Pelham had feared that unscrupulous brokers might try and buy up large numbers of lottery tickets and then sell them to the public for a huge mark-up. For that reason, nobody was allowed to buy more than twenty tickets. Leheup secretly sold to a Mr Calmel between 260 and 270 tickets under blatantly fictitious names such as 'Gileses', 'Stileses' 'Roes' and 'Does', just like the 'Mickey Mouses', 'Margaret Thatchers' and 'Ronald Reagans' signed by print-workers for shifts they never worked in pre-Wapping Fleet Street. He also bought on his own account 5,800 of the 100,000 tickets on offer at £3 each for prize money of £200,000. These were soon resold at Exchange Alley by his partner in crime, Sampson Gideon, at an outrageously inflated premium. They shared the takings.

Another concern was to ensure a prolonged sale of tickets, from 14 June to 20 October 1753, for fairness and to allow foreigners the chance to buy. To get round this legislative safeguard, Leheup fixed it that the public sale of lottery tickets was closed, on the grounds that there were none left, just six hours after it had been opened This was despite widespread newspaper advertisements that promised the public the tickets would be sold 'constantly every Day, Sundays and Holidays excepted.' His gang had bought them all up, many of them even before the 14 June starting date, in order to create a market monopoly. The devious stock jobber was able to pull these tricks by worming himself into a position where he received and processed more than half of the lottery subscriptions, instead of the quarter originally allotted to him, and controlled the marketing and advertising. For Leheup, the fraud was highly profitable; at least £40,000 went into his pocket. For many others, who bought tickets at the artificially high price and sold them for much less, it brought severe financial losses.

An avalanche of complaints forced the Commons to debate the scam on 4 December 1753. George Cooke, MP for Middlesex, opened with the charge that the 'heinous criminal' Leheup and his associates had illegally bought tickets at the lowest possible price 'to sell to the deluded people at what profit they pleased to exact.' He added that many gullible merchants and tradesmen had 'lost considerable sums of money, and some of them were utterly undone' on account of this 'secret and dark transaction.' Some MPs with sympathy for a fellow rogue, such as Henry Fox, who had himself abused public funds for private gain, supported Leheup. Others felt the whole affair was simply beneath Parliament's dignity to pursue. 'Our House of Commons – mere poachers – are piddling with the torture of Leheup, who extracted so much money out of the Lottery,' wrote the dilettante Horace Walpole, himself one of the Sloane bequest Trustees, to the artist Richard Bentley.

But at the end of the sometimes heated proceedings MPs, with the South Sea Bubble scandal still fresh in their minds, voted overwhelmingly to petition the King to instruct the attorney general to prosecute Leheup 'in the most effectual manner.' They remained unconvinced by his exclamation that the crowds besieging his office to buy tickets had simply overwhelmed him. 'People broke in upon me, above me, behind me, and before me, and in at the windows with ladders; the partitions of my desk were broke down, while I lay exposed to be plundered of all my money, which was quite open,' claimed Leheup. He was convicted of eighteen violations of the Lottery Act and fined £1,000 (£50,000 in today's money), which he immediately paid, and could afford to do so.

The lottery, however, had done its job. After expenses were deducted, £95,194 *8s 2d* was left; £20,000 bought the Sloane collection and £10,000 acquired another important collection built up by Robert Harley, first earl of Oxford. Together with the antiquary Sir Robert Cotton's collection of coins and manuscripts, which included the Lindisfarne Gospels, they laid the foundation of the British Museum. The trustees were also able to purchase Montague House in Bloomsbury to store and display them, and to invest a £30,000 capital sum to run the new museum for the next seventy years at an annual income of £1,200.

Westminster Bridge

Less controversial was an earlier lottery for Westminster Bridge. In the first half of the eighteenth century the only link between rapidly expanding Westminster and the south of the river was a flat-bottomed ferry at Horseferry Road owned by the archbishop of Canterbury. There were also boat services operated by the notoriously obstreperous Thames watermen, described as 'rude, exacting and quarrelsome' by one French visitor, Guy Miege. They campaigned ferociously against all proposals for a new bridge. Finally, the project to build a stone bridge, fifteen arches wide, a great engineering feat which inspired the Italian painter Canaletto, won royal approval and a board of commissioners, including Prime Minister Sir Robert Walpole, was appointed. They quickly agreed a lottery was the only realistic way of funding it and a series of five annual draws were organized at Stationers' Hall, starting in 1736 with 125,000 tickets being offered at £5 each and a £20,000 top prize.

Not everyone was enthusiastic. There were press complaints that the next draw, held in 1737 with prize money reduced from £525,000 to £150,000, was '46 per cent more disadvantageous' than the first; some brokers were accused of artificially inflating ticket prices; and the *Craftsman*, a publication supported by Walpole's rival Bolingbroke, alleged that every £100,000 spent on the lottery stopped at least £300,000 being circulated in the economy occasioning, 'almost a total Suppression of Trade.' The bridge took nearly twelve years to complete at a cost of £389,500, mainly from lottery money, and was finally opened to the public on 18 November 1750. Tolls ranged from two shillings for a coach and horses to a half-penny for pedestrians. Hogs went over at sixpence for twenty.

In 1754, there was a proposal to build another bridge over the Thames at Blackfriars by means of a highly complicated lottery involving life annuities. This project, it was suggested, would develop spacious streets and elegant buildings in place of 'the lay-stalls and bawdy houses, obscure pawnbrokers and alehouses, the haunts of strolling prostitutes, thieves and beggars.' It appears not to have been taken up. Perhaps the public had had enough.

YOUR MAJESTY, WAS IT REALLY
WISE TO HOCK THE CROWN JEWELS
TO BUY MORE LOTTERY TICKETS?

12

LOTTERY MANIA

LATE EIGHTEENTH CENTURY

Playing the lottery was part of a gambling mania that swept late eighteenth-century Britain. Fortunes were made and lost overnight at the gaming tables. Cockfights, horse-racing, illegal boxing matches, even maggot races, were all good for a bet. Virtually every section of society wanted to get rich quick.

A radical change in the type of prizes took place after 1769 when the Government, headed by the duke of Grafton a gambler and horse-racing fan known as 'The Turf Macaroni', mainly replaced annuities with lump cash sums. Chance thus played a much greater role in the lottery, rather like it does today.

The draw, held in public at London's Guildhall until 1802 when it was moved to Coopers' Hall, provided great theatrical entertainment Players retained one portion of their ticket. Numbered counterfoils of all tickets sold were rolled up and tied with string before being placed in a huge rotating drum (the lottery 'wheel'), six feet in diameter and eighteen inches wide. Prize tickets and blanks were placed in another wheel of the same size. Both were secured by seven separate locks and kept under guard at Whitehall, later at Somerset House on the Strand, until they were transported to the draw by a massive, horse-drawn vehicle escorted by a dismounted detachment of Life Guards. Crowds gathered to cheer on this strange procession as it trudged through the streets.

In a ceremony as precise as a Noh play, a Bluecoat boy pulled a ticket number from one wheel as, simultaneously, another boy drew a prize ticket or, much more likely, a blank, from the other wheel. A clerk stood between them to receive and shout out the numbers drawn. No less than six officials attended each wheel to enforce the government's meticulous rules for conducting the draw which took place every day from 9am to 2pm, excluding Sundays, Christmas Day and public holidays. Lottery offices, where the tickets were sold, were often open twenty-four hours.

The cost of a ticket was high. In 1797 it was £13 – but £500,000 was distributed in prize money, with three top prizes of £20,000 and the lowest £17. The government made over £250,000 and 20,000 people got prizes. News of the winning numbers were sent to remote parts by passenger coach ('The Lottery Express' could cover one hundred miles a day on some routes), horsemen racing dangerously down lanes, and to Ireland by astonishingly fast open wherries.

It was particularly popular with impoverished aristocrats such as the eighteenth-century Lady Diana Beauclerk, first born to the third duke of Marlborough. She was a highly gifted artist (though dismissed by Samuel Johnson as 'a whore') who, in the latter half of her scandalous and controversial life, plunged into poverty. A win in the State Lottery would have been her salvation. She bought a ticket on behalf of herself and her son-in-law in 1797, but their number did not come up. They tried again the following year when tickets cost £11 15s, with the same result. 'Oh dear! I am sorry to tell you the lottery ticket is – a Blank. There are nothing but Blanks (or worse) in the world, I believe', she wrote.

Diana's kinswoman, Georgiana, Duchess of Devonshire, fared better, once winning £900 in a day. But she was also always in debt. In 1787 she wrote to a friend: 'I shall be with you in the Lottery time and will have only tickets and no insurance of any kind.' Even the strictly brought up daughters of George III played. Princess Augusta wrote to her former governess: 'My sisters and me have got in the lottery [a prize of] twenty pounds and what I have got is for you.' Horace Walpole described the craze in a letter, dated 17 December 1780, to a rural friend, the Countess of Ossory:

> The reigning one [fashion] amongst the quality is to go after the Opera to the lottery offices where their Ladyships bet with the keepers. You choose any number you please; if it does not come up the next day, you pay five guineas; if it does, receive forty.

It was also quite respectable for genteel middle class women to play. Not only were they raising money for good causes such as the British Museum, but helping to fund continuing needs such as feeding the navy. The night before a big draw in 1767 a gentlewoman in Holborn, whose husband had given her a ticket, asked the congregation of her church to pray 'for the success of a person engaged in a new undertaking.' The struggling self-employed could also strike lucky. The top £10,000 prize in the Christmas lottery of 1761 was won by 'an industrious man who had laboured hard for 40 years and could barely live by his business.' He was at first told his ticket, number 37,991, was a blank but he re-checked, fortunately. On the whole, the aristocracy and professional classes could afford to lose; others could not.

The main problem was the illegal side bets, marketed as 'insurance', on which numbers would turn up. Working class people could not afford to buy tickets, which averaged £10 a throw, but they could raise the money for a shilling, 6d or 4d punt to try and win a pound if a certain lottery number came up. As the draw took more than forty days, there was an opportunity every day to try your luck, and many who could ill afford it were tempted to gamble.

As a result, social problems multiplied. In 1800, the 200,000 domestic servants working in London each spent 25s. a year on the English lottery and the same amount on the Irish lottery, making a total of £500,000 (£15 million today). According to the London magistrate, Patrick Colquhoun, these 'pampered male and female domestics in the houses of fashion and fortune' were the main group at risk since, being fed and clothed by their employers, they had disposable income. One MP recounted in the House of Commons 'the piteous tale' of his maid who had lost £200.

Wives of labourers pawned, sometimes at an extortionate rate of 850 per cent, beds and pillows, even their children's clothes and wedding rings, to play; one policeman James Bligh, based in Queen's Square in London, told a Parliamentary enquiry he had many times gone into houses where women and children 'have been almost naked'. Housekeepers, often desperate to recoup losses, stole money from their masters, or used money they had been given to pay tradesmen's bills. Children robbed their parents. In the Square Mile practically every waiter in the numerous coffee shops and taverns, hoping to follow their rich trader customers, spent their wages on tickets. Two out of three public houses had lottery societies.

Children, too, were targeted. A 1785 newspaper advertisement urged parents to buy lottery Christmas boxes for their offspring as a guinea's worth of tickets 'would afford them a fair chance of obtaining £1,600.' A popular parody titled *All the World's a Lottery* refers to what must have been a familiar scene:

> The School-boy – his Christmas box well stored –
> His face all shining with the rays of Hope –
> Creeps, in his way to School t'a Lottery Lane
> Empties his hoard and buys a Sixteenth Share

The word 'lottery' had also by then so entered the language that it became synonymous with a medley or compendium. A children's book of 1797 featured a nursery lottery office, while alphabet primers also came under the lottery imprint. A tiny (3" x 6") new lottery

A 1615 advertisment for the Virginia Company's Great Standing Lottery, showing off the glittering prizes on offer and the two Indians shipped over to help publicise the draw.

Pickpockets work the crowd at the Guildhall draw in 1751.

Life Guards escorting the lottery wheels from Somerset House to Coopers' Hall.

Hogarth's surprisingly pedestrian allegory of the lottery (1724).

Hogarth's savage 1721 satire of the South Sea Bubble depicts a matrimonial raffle (top left) with women queuing up to play for husbands.

A priestess draws out a bean from an ealy Greek lottery (vase painting, c. 500 B.C.).

A satire on the Bluecoat boys at the lottery by George Cruikshank (steel engraving, 1817). Desperate for money, he also illustrated lottery advertisements.

Charles 'Patch' Price, crooked lottery operator of the eighteenth century and master of disguises.

Nineteenth-century lottery advertisement using innovative matchstick men.

Advertisement from Thomas Bish, celebrated nineteenth-century lottery entrepreneur.

Enigmatic lottery handbill from the 1800s.

Advertisement for England's 'last ever lottery' in 1826 when state lotteries were abolished.

Whipping up support for the last lottery.

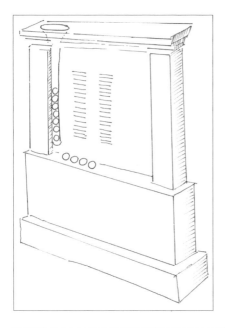

Athenian allotment machine (reconstruction).

The lucky draw at Coopers' Hall (Pugin and Rowlandson aquatint, 1810).

book of birds and beasts 'for children to learn their letters by as soon as they can speak', was published in Newcastle in 1771, with exquisite woodcuts by the illustrator Thomas Bewick. These publications were thus, unintentionally, part of a general lottery branding.

There were many individual tragedies. Entrepreneur Christopher Bartholomew owned the Angel Inn at Islington, tea gardens, and the largest number of haystacks in London, still a rural capital in 1790. He swanked around in a carriage and spent 2,000 guineas a day on betting and buying lottery tickets, often winning and celebrating with free breakfasts for his customers. At last his luck turned, he lost heavily and sold haystack after haystack to finance his gambling. He lived in poverty, begging old clothes and scraps of food from friends. Then, in 1807, he had a hunch on a number, borrowed the money for a ticket from a friend, and won £20,000 – but he promptly lost it all again. Bartholomew died, destitute, in a garret at Angel Court in Windmill Street, Soho in March 1809 at the age of sixty-eight.

In his autobiography, the radical reformer Francis Place catalogued the lottery losses of his father who, bedridden with gout during the 1791 draw, was unable reach a secret drawer in his bureau where he hid numerous tickets. He had to reveal their existence to his son, and instructed him to take them to the lottery office. They were all blanks. His entire capital had gone, leaving the family destitute. Place wrote: 'no human being can conceive the distress of my poor mother'. At the age of sixty, she became a washerwoman, working from 4am until midnight every day in order to feed her husband and children.

Newspapers reported suicides with depressing regularity. One gentleman, ruined by lottery speculation, shot himself in a Westminster street in 1787. He left a note cursing 'the head that planned, and the heart that executed' the baneful, destructive plan of a lottery. A footman, under the influence of a dream, spent his life savings on two tickets which came up blanks. He killed himself and his mistress found a pathetic note saying that as soon as he received the money he would marry his bad-tempered girlfriend, Grace Towers, but treat her as a servant:

Every morning she shall get me a mug of strong beer, with a toast,
nutmeg, and sugar in it; then I will sleep till ten, after which I will
have a large sack posset …

Theatrical entrepreneur Lord Barrymore was luckier; he dreamt of
a number, bet on it, and won £10,000. People were spectacularly
careless with their tickets. So many were losing them in 1710 that
Parliament passed an act, 'for the relief of persons who have not
claimed their lottery tickets in due time.' Desperate advertisements
appeared in *The Spectator* magazine. 'Return to Mr Tho Shuttleworth
at Jonathan's Coffee-house in Change-Alley 10s reward.'

In 1757, according to the *Gentleman's Magazine*, 'Mr Keys, late
clerk to Cotton and Co, who had absented himself ever since
the 7th of October, the day the £10,000 prize was drawn in the
Lottery (supposed to be his property) was found in the streets
raving mad, having been robbed of his pocket-book and ticket.'

Winning did not always guarantee happiness. Mr Alder, a publican and cooper from Abingdon in Berkshire, bought ticket No.
3379 for the 19 November draw of the 1767 Lottery and it came
up against odds of 35,000 to one. He won a colossal fortune of
£20,000 (the equivalent of £1 million today).

Generous to a fault, Mr Alder began throwing his unexpected
fortune around. He gave £100 to the broker from Barnes and
Golightly who sped down by express coach from his office near
London's Royal Exchange to tell him the good news. This the
broker delivered with expert psychology. Instead of blurting it
out, he broke it very cautiously raising the sum won by degrees
from £20 to £20,000; even so the fortunate winner, a sixty-year-
old grandfather, still 'exhibited some appearance of shock and
trembling.' He soon recovered and started his spending spree.

As all the church bells of Abingdon pealed in rejoicing, he invited
all his neighbours into his little public house, called The Mitre, called
for a wet mop to wipe out all their liquor debts chalked up on a
blackboard and promised them all as much drink as they could take
as well as a share of the money. Even the bell ringers were given a

guinea each and huge quantities of ale. But the excited Mr Alder did not stop there. He lent one of his customers, a poor cobbler, enough money to buy leather to stock his stall so full that he would be unable to get into it to work. He promised a Mr Blewitt, owner of the Abingdon coach which brought down the considerate broker, a set of the most expensive horses on the market and brand new bodywork, on condition it displayed the Cooper's Arms and the number of his winning ticket. He gave large sums to the two Bluecoat boys who drew the top prize, just three days into the two-month draw. Nor did he neglect the local poor. He gave them new clothes and roast meat. As *The London Evening Post* reported: 'In a word he displayed a noble liberality and made everybody welcome.' Mrs Alder, who at first thought news of the win was a practical joke, took a different view. According to the newspaper, she believed it a misfortune which 'would now certainly be their ruin, as she feared her husband would give away all they had in the world.' She was voicing a common fear which the anonymous correspondent 'D.T.' reflected in the *Gentleman's Magazine*: 'the monstrous prizes of £10,000 and £5,000 are a perfect nuisance ... they are more fit to turn the brains of a poor man than to help him.'

It is not known whether the worried wife was proved right, although it is on record that a kindly neighbour became so concerned by Alder's mental state and the hordes of grasping gold-diggers besieging The Mitre that he spirited him away for a long tour. As a more encouraging sidelight on human nature, the publican's generosity set a good example for other winners; the following Saturday, another Abingdon resident, Mr Daston, won a £2,000 prize with ticket number 40,193, and promptly promised to distribute three roasted oxen to the needy.

By 1800, more than 400 unlicensed lottery houses, known as 'Little Go's' and run by well-known criminals like Charles Price, were scattered throughout London from Islington to Clerkenwell. *The Times* described their proprietors as 'needy beggars, desperate swindlers, gamblers, sharpers, notorious thieves, and common convicted felons.' Earlier the total was even higher. According to a 1787 newspaper report there were 1,500 illegal premises 'not paying a farthing to the Government', unlike the official offices which from 1779 each paid £50 year for a licence. But the unofficial dens were very popular and continued to operate on virtually the same scale as the state lotteries. On 11 August 1795, magistrates in St James's, increasingly alarmed by the impact on the poorer population of the capital, ordered a crackdown. Warrants were issued for raids on houses in Golden Square, Soho, King Street, and many other locations, where invariably scores of people were found playing.

Raids, £500 fines and continual official harassment, all proved futile. Rather like inner-city crack houses today, the clandestine lottery houses made too much money to care much about the financial penalties for issuing numbers. A 1796 report estimated that they illegally received £1,200,000 (£36 million today) for each drawing of the Irish lottery and £2 million (£60 million today) for the English lottery, making a profit of between twenty-five to thirty per cent. The owners even had their own trade association. This met regularly as a committee at an Oxford Street public house three times a week during draws to co-ordinate measures, including bribery, to thwart the magistrates and police.

Some other, more strategic measures did begin to work. Side bets on the official lottery, carried out at the Guildhall, were possible only because the Corporation of the City of London sold places for the draw. Runners employed by the illegal lottery houses were thus able to gain entry, take down the numbers as they emerged from the wheel and announce them at regular intervals. However, after 1793, nobody was allowed in save officials and clerks working for the licensed lottery offices.

Nine years later the illegal operators were reined in even tighter when Parliament decreed, in the 1802 Lottery Act, that the draw must take only eight days instead of forty-two. Despite these reforms, pressure began to mount for the total abolition of the lottery. Formidable opponents began to line up, including a man looking for a new challenge: the slave trade abolitionist William Wilberforce.

I WANT TO FREE THE
'SLAVES TO FORTUNE' TOO

13

ARCH OPPONENT
WILLIAM WILBERFORCE

At 4am on the morning of 24 February 1807 the House of Commons voted overwhelmingly by 283 votes to 16 to abolish the slave trade. It was the magnificent climax of a remorseless eighteen-year campaign on the part of the abolitionists led by the Yorkshire MP, William Wilberforce. As they celebrated in his room in Parliament, William turned to his friend and fellow legislator Henry Thornton and asked playfully: 'Well, Henry, what shall we abolish next?' The reply came swiftly: 'The Lottery, I think.'

They succeeded – though the necessary legislation took even longer than the law to ban trading in slaves. Wilberforce welcomed reforms such as preventing the illegal betting on numbers, removing the corrupt Inspector General of Lotteries, Thomas Wood, and the 1809 decision that the entire lottery must be drawn in one day. Yet such positive steps did not satisfy this complicated and contradictory character, who saw the issue in uncompromising terms. 'The thing is wrong in principle,' he told his reformist friend, Samuel Roberts.

The lottery was simply one of many abolitionist causes he supported. They included bull baiting, boy chimney sweeps, military flogging, hanging, harsh prison conditions, adultery, and even the 'indecent practice' of sea bathing at Brighton. His chance to kick-start the lottery campaign came when a select committee of the House of Commons, chaired by Sir Samuel Whitbread, produced two reports in 1808 on how far the new lottery laws had stopped malpractice and fraud. Little attempt was made to publicise the findings, and only the barest summary was published in one or two newspapers. However, evidence from magistrates, policemen, clergymen, tradesmen, pawnbrokers and employers convinced Wilberforce and his group of about twenty-five Parliamentary supporters, nicknamed The Saints, that a total ban was the only solution.

Many of the horror stories recounted by London magistrates such as Patrick Colquhoun and Robert Baker, long-standing opponent of lotteries, were all the more convincing as daily, on the bench, they had to deal with the fall-out from the game. A widow, who earned £400 a year running a silk-dyeing company, was ruined when her foreman, who received just £33 a year in wages, began spending £300 to £400 a week on the lottery using her name for credit. The stress killed him and he died insolvent, leaving huge bills for her which she could pay only at the rate of three shillings in the pound. The widow went into an almshouse and died four months later.

A coachman, having won one-sixteenth of a £20,000 prize, became addicted to the lottery, spent all his money on it and went mad. 'He has since recovered his senses, but his wife fretted herself to death,' the Rev. William Gurney, Minister of the Free Chapel of St Giles, told MPs. Another clergyman, the Rev. Brownlow Ford, chaplain to the inmates of Newgate prison, said 'When I have put the question to malefactors, "What first drove you to crime?", the answer has been: "it was poverty from buying and insuring in the lottery."'

Wilberforce, who was quick to seize these accounts as ammunition, was encouraged by the unequivocal way Whitbread's second, substantive report condemned the game. The MPs concluded:

> The foundation of the Lottery is so radically vicious, that Your Committee feel convinced that under no system of regulations that can be devised will it be possible for Parliament to adopt it as an efficacious source of Revenue, and, at the same time, divest it of all the Evils and Calamities of which it has, hitherto, proved so baneful a source.

But it took years to convince Parliament, which was concerned by the burden of heavy taxation and huge debts on account of the wars with Napoleon. Ministers were reluctant to give up such a lucrative source of revenue at a time when they were struggling to restore a badly damaged economy, and at a time when the French dictator was also boosting his economy through his own expanding state lottery. The campaigning Yorkshireman put forward strong arguments against lotteries, but an attempt by the Saints to have them banned was rejected so decisively by MPs that he became discouraged. 'Where there is no prospect of success...', he began a letter in 1816.

For the next eighteen months he was preoccupied with other crusades. Meanwhile, anti-lottery propagandists poured out pamphlets and books, often spoiling their case with language even more extreme than that used about slave trading. In his tract *The State Lottery, A Dream*, Samuel Roberts denounces the Bluecoat boys as 'servants of the devil', and the lottery as 'one of the vilest and most abominable measures that ever dishonoured the annals of the world.' The poet James Montgomery, a nineteenth-century McGonagall, ends his poem *Lottery Wheels* with a similar purple passage:

> But O be Lottery wheels afar!
> I'll die by torture, war, disease,
> I'll die – by any Wheels but these!

Despite evangelical fanaticism, support for a ban began, very slowly, to grow. Wilberforce resumed his campaign. When the Lottery Act came up for renewal in 1818, Henry Brooke Parnell MP suggested the following epitaph be inscribed on the tomb of the chancellor:

> Here lies the Right Hon. Nicholas Vansittart, once Chancellor of the Exchequer, the patron of Bible Societies, the builder of Churches, a friend to the education of the poor, an encourager of Savings Banks, and – a supporter of lotteries!

The following year Lord Lyttelton moved a motion in the House declaring that state lotteries were injurious to people's morals, weakened the will to work, thus diminishing public revenues, and led to even worse forms of gambling. Bluntly, his motion concluded: 'That this House, therefore, will no longer authorize the establishment of State lotteries under any system of regulations whatever.' Vansittart counter-argued that the public would suffer if such a major addition to state finances was abandoned without replacement and that the lottery merely reflected the wish for a flutter and was not the root cause of gambling. Wilberforce replied that such an argument 'might be brought forward to justify the farming of the public stews, by which perhaps £500,000 might be obtained.'

Lyttelton's motion was rejected by 133 votes to 84; five similar abolitionist motions since 1816 had also failed by large majorities. Yet over the next two years it became clear that time was running out for the draw.

Wilberforce, in failing health from colitis relieved only by an uncomfortable steel girdle and opium, still managed to struggle to the House to argue his case. Edmund Burke had rated him, even as a novice MP, as one of the most brilliant natural orators since Demosthenes, and his anti-lottery speeches in the twilight of his Parliamentary career were as effective as ever. He was now also greatly helped by the fact that the economic slump of 1819–1822, when real wages fell by one fifth, had dramatically cut ticket sales; the average net annual profit for 1816–1823 (£202,500) was half what it was for 1802–1815 (£407,400). At the same time, lottery expenses were increasing; of the £10 million gross income raised between 1810 and 1820, sixty-eight per cent had to be set aside for prize money. The decline in revenue also coincided with an increasing feeling among treasury officials that the entire system, with its confusing and probably inaccurate sets of accounts, time-consuming annual negotiations with lottery contractors and institutional corruption, had become an inefficient, bureaucratic monster.

So, for a mix of moral and economic reasons, Lord Liverpool's government became convinced that the lottery had had its day. As all lotteries were established by specific statute, no abolition bill was necessary. The 1823 Lottery Act, passed on 9 July, simply made provision to discontinue the draw. Lottery commissioners and their offices were to stay for another three years longer to allow them to wind up outstanding business and to organise one final fling.

A Rowlandson cartoon appeared called *The Chance Seller of the Exchequer Putting an Extinguisher on Lotteries*. It shows the chancellor, Robinson, placing an extinguisher on Fortune's head (symbol for the lottery), while Wilberforce, seizing coins and prizes says: 'Persevere and the Saints shall praise you.' The abolitionists, with a little help from the Treasury and the economic situation, had won again. Evangelists everywhere rejoiced. 'Another triumph of sound moral principle over fiscal policy', trumpeted *The Christian Observer*.

The Last Draw

The 1823 Lottery Act not only banned lotteries in Britain, but the sale of foreign lotteries. It did, however, permit one final drawing, postponed a number of times, which was eventually completed in 1826 among raucous scenes.

A huge publicity campaign was mounted in the weeks before the draw, planned for Tuesday 18 July 1826. Thousands of hand-bills dramatically describing it as 'positively the last lottery that will ever be drawn in England' were distributed. Full-page adver-tisements using lottery alphabets and humorous verses appeared in newspapers. Processions of liveried men with sandwich boards and poles, and men with purple silk banners embossed in large gold letters paraded about. They were accompanied by bands of trumpets, clarionets and horns, a painted carriage representing the lottery wheel drawn by two dappled grey horses, and a square carriage surmounted by a gilt imperial crown. All the boards and notices carried the same message: 'all lotteries end for ever on Tuesday next!'. Rival brokers put out innovative and ingenious promotional material; their offices were decorated with lanterns, trumpeters blared their way through the streets, and gaily dressed carts proclaimed the launch of one scheme or another. It was an advertising revolution.

The draw was postponed, however, by treasury order until Thursday 18 October because the contractors told officials they needed more time to get rid of unsold tickets. Yet, at the same time, they were promoting the idea among the public that tickets were in great demand by arbitrarily raising the price.

The parades continued: one comical contraption, octagonally shaped, twenty to thirty feet high and covered with different col-oured lottery papers, whose driver and horse 'seemed as dull as though they were attending a solemn funeral,' according to the artist commissioned to sketch the scene, was heckled and then attacked, as it weaved its eccentric way along a street in Holborn. 'It entered Monmouth Street, that den of filth and rags, where so great a number of young urchins gathered together in a few min-utes as to be astonishing,' he wrote. They pelted the ungainly cart with stones and oyster shells, while elsewhere men with lottery bills on poles also obstructed the streets and were shooed away by the beadles. Complaints mounted about advertising horns being blown late at night.

The draw took place at Coopers' Hall, traditional venue since 1802 following objections to the use of the Guildhall. As had been the custom, the 'wheels' (lottery boxes) were drawn on sledges, and escorted by fourteen soldiers to the crowded hall. As usual, the Bluecoat boys from Christ's Hospital drew the tickets, receiving a shilling each for their work. It was all over in less than ninety minutes, and few prizes appear to have been won.

The Times marked the demise of the state lottery after an uninterrupted period of 132 years with a well-balanced editorial. It pointed out lotteries raised revenues for the Treasury totalling between £250,000 and £300,000 each year and so it was now up to those who had called for the ban to provide for the deficiency. However, it also concluded that the public mainly welcomed the end of a system which had caused so much misery.

The fact that more than half the tickets remained unsold justified Parliament's belief that people no longer supported it. In the annual Harlequin pantomime at Covent Garden later that year, the lottery took pride of place in a scene showing its ghost 'flying over the ruins of his trade'. Contemporary ditties celebrated the victory; one mocked the lottery's most celebrated entrepreneur Thomas Bish and declared:

Bish, our Leviathian, is gone half mad
And looks as dismal as a blank drawn ticket

THEY'RE THE SAME, REALLY—
PROMISING THE EARTH, THEN
LETTING YOU DOWN

14

PIONEER OF ADVERTISING

THOMAS BISH

Thomas Bish, a prototype for Britain's favourite tycoon Richard Branson, was a publicity-mad lottery contractor and pioneer of modern advertising techniques who eventually ended up as a respectable Member of Parliament. He brilliantly exploited the lottery fever that raged in Britain until the 1826 ban, operating two of the most well-known lottery houses at 4 Cornhill and 9 Charing Cross. They were boastfully described as 'the luckiest offices in the Kingdom'. No wonder so many racehorses were named after him.

His father, also called Thomas Bish, started in the lottery business in 1778 and became a licensed office keeper in 1790. Both were showmen, but it was Bish Junior who had the flair that would make him a B-list celebrity of the day. He was just seventeen years old when he first helped his father organise a state lottery with his business partner, the much older stockbroker Sir

James Branscomb. The draw, which took place on 22 February 1796, worked well, with £500,000 in prizes and a net gain to the Exchequer of £245,208, 18s, 11d. Two years later the Bishes set up on their own, taking over Branscomb's London offices and starting a branch in Manchester.

Soon there were branches or agents, including booksellers, printers, hatters, even goldsmiths, in every main town in Britain and Ireland. From 1799 to the last draw in 1826, the Bish brand dominated the scene, overshadowing the other brokers, such as Pidding, Sivewright, Eyton, Hazard and Goodluck.

Bish Junior, who increasingly ran the business some years before his father's death in 1815, had a finger in many business pies; he jointly bought the loss-making London pleasure ground Vauxhall Gardens in 1821, and set up as a wine merchant, with the London Wine Company. His partner in both enterprises was a tall, good-looking printer from Bristol called Frederick Gye who had a shop at Broad Street in the City of London. He won a lucrative contract for printing state lottery tickets and also printed Bish's lottery posters and advertisements. On the eve before one draw, Bish gave him a batch of unsold tickets and Gye won a prize of £30,000. Today, lottery employees and contractors as well as their relatives are strictly forbidden to enter the draw.

Success turned Bish into a society figure 'of great attraction', according to one newspaper; he lived in style in a grand house in St James' Square, he had the ear of government ministers, became a prominent member of the Garrick Club, was feted at business functions and was portrayed in etchings. He was also a man of great wealth. Lottery operators usually made a profit on sales, clear of expenses, of about thirty-three per cent, compared to less than one per cent now. If a lottery sold particularly well, they could make £60,000 (£1,800,000 today), though this was not guaranteed and there was always the risk of a loss. That was why lottery offices often changed hands for whopping 'goodwill' payments of £10,000 (£300,000 today). The gap between rich men like Bish and the working class London poor was vividly illustrated in 1820 when fourteen-year-old John Wotton, errand boy to Bish and Gye, was prosecuted for stealing teaspoons from the two entrepreneurs and sentenced to seven years' transportation.

Bish's advertising genius must have come from his father. Once, within hours of a burglary at his house at No. 4 Cornhill, Bish Senior printed and displayed handbills listing the silver tea things stolen and offering a £50 reward for information. This swiftly led to the capture of the thief, James 'Putty' Parsey, a glazier's apprentice who had been fitting glass at the house. He was tried and sentenced to death at the Old Bailey.

An outrageous self-publicist, Bish Junior promoted himself through posters, leaflets with imaginative matchstick figures, sandwich men, torchlight processions, and horse-drawn Heath Robinson contraptions. These brash methods often caused offence: the press campaigned against 'papers affixed to churches and errand carts – held up on poles at the corners of streets – and distributed by the meanest of mankind in the narrowest passages of the town.' More effective were advertisements printed in both national and more than 100 provincial newspapers, written by ingenious copywriters including the diarist Charles Lamb and illustrated by the artist George Cruikshank. They appealed blatantly to greed.

One handbill, *THE ALCHYMIST*, promised 'a House and Land, and Carriage.' The *Lottery Alphabet*, said:

A stands for All who for Affluence wish,
B means Be sure Buy a Ticket of BISH,
C Cash in plenty by BISH you may gain …

Another declared:

The Bish for my money, I say,
The likes of him never was known, sir.

No-one could accuse him of false modesty.

Generally, adverts from competitors were pedestrian, though they eventually caught on and imitated his innovative visuals. For the New Year State Lottery, which began drawing on 21 January 1821 for prizes of up to 21,000 guineas, his advertisements featured verse-speaking colourful portraits of characters from plays being staged in London over Christmas. Queen Dollallolla from *Tom Thumb* says:

How now? The Prizes to be paid in Guineas!
If you don't try, you are confounded ninnies.

Always with a sharp eye to the main chance, the ingenious marketing man invariably found a publicity angle. The visit to Britain of the Persian envoy was cheekily exploited in a song which lists his visits to George III, the opera, Bank of England and climaxes with a trip 'To Bish's, a lottery ticket to buy'. In 1811, he cashed in on the three royal weddings that year; even the 1820 trial of Queen Caroline was used for a lottery handbill.

Bish took care to include Wales, Scotland and Ireland in his strategy. A St David's Day lottery drawn on Saturday 1 March 1817, with only 3,000 tickets and a top prize of £15,000, was promoted as the 'smallest lottery ever known'. Handbills in both Welsh and English were distributed in towns like Caernarvon and at Welsh Fairs in London. One, *The Maid of Llangollen*, explains why a Welsh couple bought a ticket:

They had kisses in plenty – but what were all these,
For kisses would not supply bread to the cheese.
So John Morgan and Winifred both felt a wish
For a Lottery Ticket from THOMAS AP BISH

He also targeted sectors such as middle class women; many puffs regularly appeared in monthly advertising supplements to *The Lady's Magazine*.

Bish was much more than an advertising spiv. He was an effective lottery lobbyist, once persuading the Chancellor Vansittart to drop a scheme whereby the Government could deprive a lottery contractor of his licence without allowing the opportunity for a defence. His powerful intellect marshalled cogent arguments against Wilberforce, though it was another lottery contractor, H.E.Smith, who organised the rescue plan put to government when the lottery system began breaking down in 1823. Maybe the contractors no longer regarded him as such a safe pair of hands; only two years earlier he had been involved in a ferocious slanging match in the media with Messrs Carroll, Hazard and Company, each accusing the other of fraud.

Nowhere is his subtle mind more evident than in his persuasive 'manifesto' to the public published on the eve of abolition. It stands today as an effective defence of financial lotteries. Bish pointing out that the State gains half a million pounds in revenue from lotteries, argues that reforms prevent the poorest punters being exploited and defrauded. Then he gets to the nub. 'As it is at present conducted, the Lottery is a voluntary tax,' he says, 'contributed to only by those who can afford it, and collected without trouble or expense; one by which many branches of the revenue are considerably aided, and by means of which hundreds of persons find employment.'

He ends with a sly dig at the legislators who voted for a ban:

> To stake patrimonial estates at hazard or ecarte, in the purlieus of St.James's, is merely amusement, but to purchase a ticket in the Lottery, by which a man may gain an estate at a trifling risk, is – immoral!

Members of Parliament did not take kindly to this and, shortly afterwards, when Bish was himself elected MP for Leominster, defeating the banker Rowland Stephenson, they took their revenge by unseating him on the grounds of being a lottery contractor. In February 1827, MPs granted an election petition from Stephenson, regarded as 'a rich London banker as safe as or safer than the Bank of England,' that he be returned for the seat. They may have regretted not sticking with Bish; eighteen months later, and amid huge publicity, Stephenson absconded to Savannah, Georgia, with £58,000 in cash from his Lombard Street banking house, causing it to crash Barings-style.

Meanwhile, his old friend, Frederick Gye, became MP for Chippenham. Eventually, in 1832, Bish was again elected for Leominster, representing the constituency uninterruptedly until he stood down in 1837. He died two days after Christmas day 1842 at the age of sixty-three. An obituary noted: 'Mr Bish is more well-known than the Prime Minister of England.' As an MP, this now forgotten figure proved a surprisingly public-spirited, energetic and forceful reformer; he voted against the Corn Laws, supported extending the ballot and promoted other Parliamentary reforms. One of his many campaigns was the need for the Bank of England to design banknotes in such a way that it was much harder to forge them – undoubtedly prompted by his experience with lottery tickets.

WAKE UP, CHARLES— YOU'RE ONLY DREAMING

15

MYSTICAL VIEW

CHARLES LAMB

A key supporter of Bish's ill-fated campaign was a brilliant diarist, manic depressive, alcoholic, and early admirer of the visionary poet William Blake: Charles Lamb. His vision of the lottery as 'this most generous diffuser of universal happiness' was practically mystical, and gives an artist's insight as to why it will always be with us. This was later replicated, though slightly differently, in George Orwell's novel *Nineteen Eighty-Four*. His bleak look into the future depicts the lottery as the lifeline of the proletariat, 'their delight, their folly, their anodyne, their intellectual stimulant.'

Charles, a regular player, had been fascinated by the lottery ever since his father had taken him to Guildhall. Here, hoisted upon a servant's shoulder, the sensitive young child sat spellbound watching a blindfolded young boy from his own school, Christ's Hospital, draw the winning tickets from lottery wheels housed in huge iron cabinets.

The scene, as stolid officials announced without emotion the lucky winners to an excited crowd, clearly fired his imagination. From an early age he loved colour, excitement and drama. Visits to the theatre, trips to the Tower of London to see the bears, wolves, lions and tigers then kept there, his fascination with witches, love of magic and his lifelong special empathy with children, all contributed to his belief in the superiority of the imagination over mere rationality. 'Man is not a creature of pure reason', he declares in his essay, *Mrs Battle's Opinions on Whist*, which elevates betting on cards into a drama of 'other-worldliness.' This desire to escape from a brutal, materialistic world manifested itself in lunatic late-night drinking bouts with Samuel Coleridge in the Salutation and Cat in Newgate Street, 'A most foul stye,' according to George IV's Poet Laureate, Robert Southey. Rising at 5am with a hangover, Lamb would knock out jokes at sixpence a time for newspapers, before going off to the day job as a glorified clerk in the accounts department of the East India House, where he worked for thirty-three years, perched on a high stool scribbling away with a goose quill details of goods brought in on the latest East Indiaman into London docks. The sheer, mind-numbing tedium of office life as a bean-counter coordinating shipments of bandages, screws, tents and other supplies to India must have made him yearn for a more romantic life.

Nowhere is this more evident than in his powerful lament for the passing of the state lottery. Called *The Illustrious Defunct* and published in the *New Monthly Magazine* of January 1825, it is one of the most convincing tracts in favour of lotteries ever written. This is not on account of his argument that they are a voluntary tax. 'Never have we joined,' he wrote, 'in the senseless clamour which condemned the only tax whereto we became voluntary contributors, the only resource which gave the stimulus without the danger or infatuation of gambling.' Many others, from Bish to Camelot, have hammered that point.

Neither is it because of Lamb's warning off the impact of abolition on the fledgling advertising industry which had emerged to promote the game; one of the first advertising agents was James White, a school friend of Lamb who had persuaded him to write copy for lottery newspaper advertisements. His sister, Mary Lamb, wrote to Sarah Hazlitt in 1809 saying

> A man in the India House has resigned, by which Charles will get twenty pounds a year; and White has prevailed on him to write some more lottery-puffs. If that ends up in smoke, the twenty pounds is a sure card, and has made us very joyful.

Much later, in 1825, the diarist's friend Thomas Hood wrote in the *London Magazine*:

> It is pretty well-known that a celebrated prose writer of the present time [taken to be Lamb] was induced by Bish to try his hand at those little corner delicacies of a News-paper, – the Lottery puffs.

One lottery ad, probably by Lamb, was placed by White's firm in *Bell's Weekly Messenger* just before Christmas 1806. It read:

> A SEASONABLE HINT, – Christmas gifts of innumerable descriptions will now pervade this whole kingdom. It is submitted whether any present is capable of being attended with so much good to a dutiful son, an amiable daughter, an industrious apprentice, or a faithful servant, as that of a SHARE of a LOTTERY TICKET, in a scheme in which the smallest share may gain near two thousand pounds.

Hardly the standard of *Essays of Elia*, the collection of essays that made his name, but it helped his meagre East India House wages.

Lamb heaped praise on his fellow marketeers and regretted their passing:

> They will be the first, as they will assuredly be the last, who fully developed the resources of that ingenious art, who cajoled and

decoyed the most suspicious and wary reader into a perusal of their advertisements by devices of endless variety and cunning; who baited their lurking schemes with midnight murders, ghost stories, crim-cons, bon-mots, balloons, dreadful catastrophes, and every diversity of joy and sorrow to catch newspaper-gudgeons. Ought not such talents to be encouraged? Verily the abolitionists have much to answer for!

But the most compelling argument in his beautifully written lament is that the lottery is a truly spiritual force, capable of liberating the adult imagination, a suitable view indeed from this Peter Pan-like figure. Lamb goes well beyond the conventional role of the draw in creating sudden wealth into a celebration of its ability to appeal, in an almost elemental way, to the soul.

This is what he wrote about the enjoyment it gave

> Let it be termed a delusion; a fool's paradise is better than the wise man's Tartarus: be it branded an Ignis fatuus, it was at least a benevolent one, which instead of beguiling its followers into swamps, caverns, and pitfalls, allured them on with all the blandishments of enchantment to a Garden of Eden, an ever-blooming Elysium of delight.

Warning that materialism would now replace imagination, he continued:

> Life will now become a flat, prosaic routine of matter-of-fact, and sleep itself, erst so prolific of numerical configurations and mysterious stimulants to lottery adventure, will be disfurnished of its figures and stimulants.

According to Lamb, the true 'magic of the Lottery' was its ability to give hope and feed the dreams of so many who were otherwise condemned to a humdrum existence. This was later echoed by a French story in which a lottery supporter says:

Every time I give my five franc piece for a quarter of a ticket, I receive more satisfaction than if I had spent it at the Restaurateur, for I purchase the privilege of raising castles for the next twenty-four hours.

Lamb's argument for escapism was this:

The true mental epicure always purchased his ticket early, and postponed enquiry into its fate to the last possible moment, during the whole of which intervening period he had an imaginary twenty thousand locked up in his desk, – and was not this well worth all the money? Who would scruple to give twenty pounds interest for even the ideal enjoyment of as many thousands during two or three months? … we can no longer succeed in such splendid failures; all our changes of making such a miss have vanished with the last of the Lotteries.

Lamb was, as we know, mistaken. It was not the last lottery and the PR and advertising men were not the last of their breed. Late in the next century their professional descendants resurrected, in the UK National Lottery, promotions on a scale that the nineteenth-century industry would have certainly applauded, but probably would have found hard to believe.

FATHER, I CANNOT TELL A LIE...
...I WILL SHARE MY WINNINGS
WITH YOU.

16

NEVER TOLD A LIE?

GEORGE WASHINGTON

When George Washington, first president of the United States and commander-in-chief during the War of Independence, was a small boy just six years old, his parents gave him a shiny new axe as a birthday present. The future world statesman happily set about chopping up anything that came his way, including a beautiful English cherry tree, pride and joy of the family's Virginian orchard. 'George,' said his distraught father 'do you know who killed the tree?' Young George, immediately and bravely, cried out: 'I can't tell a lie, Pa; you know I can't tell a lie. I did cut it with my hatchet.' So goes the famous tale, as related by one of his early biographers, Parson Weems.

But was the great man as straight as history supposes? He married a rich widow yet managed to incur huge debts; he seems to have fiddled his expenses, and let his personal money affairs fall into chaos. During one short period, from September

1775 to March 1776, he is reported to have spent more than $6,000 on alcohol alone; all paid for by Congress until they discovered his excessive spending and stopped the allowance. For such a symbol of republicanism, he exhibited some distinctly capitalist tendencies. In 1778, he wanted 'to get quit' of 317 uneconomic black slaves on his Mount Vernon Estate; six years later, he hounded through the courts, demanding the rent or eviction of some poverty-stricken farmers of an obscure religious sect who were cultivating plots on land he owned in western Pennsylvania. They were unaware there was an absentee owner called George Washington, then the most famous man in the world. His diary for 14 September 1784 records grumpily: 'This day also the People who lives on my land on Millers Run came here to set forth their pretensions to it.' Given his liking for money, it was inevitable that he became a great fan of lotteries, promoting them as well as playing them – and winning big prizes with suspicious regularity.

This may have been due to bloody-mindedness against the British, whom he had spent eight years fighting to free the new nation from the imperial yoke. The London government, stubbornly ignoring the fact that virtually all its American colonies used lotteries very effectively to boost their finances, tried to ban them in 1769. Eight years earlier, the English agent for Massachusetts warned that Lord Sandys, British trade minister under the recently crowned monarch George III, had 'inveighed against them [lotteries] as mischievous in their nature, and destructive to labour and industry.' Since Britain itself had for years held annual lotteries, this was seen as highly unreasonable and hypocritical. What was sauce for the goose was evidently not sauce for the gander. The colonies were ordered not to authorise any draws without the Crown's permission on the grounds that 'great frauds and abuses have been committed.' The real reason for this nanny state approach to the young offspring was almost certainly a desire to tighten control of the American possessions following the French and Indian war.

So it must have been with great delight that Washington put up the proverbial two fingers to the defeated British and sanctioned lottery schemes, which soared to a total of 100 in the first thirteen years of independence. 'Every part of the United States abounds in lotteries,' declared Boston's *Columbian Centinel* on 22 January 1791. The *Pennsylvania Mercury* agreed saying, 'the lottery mania appears to rage with uncommon violence.'

The father of the nation appears to have been always attracted to the game. His papers reveal vividly his lifelong enthusiasm for lotteries which, with his support, made an enormous contribution to developing America's educational system and internal transport. In 1767, he bought twenty tickets at £5 each of 10,000 advertised for sale in a raffle to dispose of Colonel Bryd's land on the River James, and later entered an agreement with nine other men to purchase jointly another 100 tickets. When the draw was held in Williamsburg the following year, he won on his own with ticket no. 4965, a half-acre lot in what was to be laid out as the town of Manchester. He also won one-tenth shares in prizes drawn by his partners, including four two-acre lots on the Manchester site and two one hundred-acre lots in Henrico County north of the James River. Years later, however, in 1784, he complained in a letter to his lawyer Edmund Randolph: 'I have never received an iota of these prizes', adding he had heard the jointly owned parcels of land had been sold for very little. Randolph confirmed the selling off, but said he had no idea of the value of Washington's own lot. Strangely, five years later, both men seemed to have forgotten about this exchange as they had further convoluted correspondence wondering what had happened to the prizes.

Washington's other gambles were much more straightforward. He won £5 in a 1763 scheme, another £16 in the York lottery of 1766, ventured £5, 10s in an unidentified lottery in 1760, and paid John Potts, a friend and local storeowner, £4, 4s in part payment for twenty tickets at six shillings each in Virginia's 1790 lottery for paving the streets of Alexandria. The balance was paid from money won in earlier draws, from a standing account he had set up specially to play the game.

Even in the midst of fighting the British, he still found time to fret about his tickets. From his military camp at Middlebrook he sent a letter in February 1779 to John Mitchell, deputy quartermaster-general in Philadelphia, requisitioning china, candlesticks, tablecloths and a hat. In it he tucked some lottery tickets with the plea: 'Please to examine if any of the inclosed tickets have come up Prizes.' Within days Mitchell replied reassuringly: 'Yesterday all your tickets were in the Wheel but one is a blank; the Lottery is very rich and much in favour of the Tickets not yet drawn.'

As a sponsor, the president was equally energetic, moving a bill in the Virginia House of Burgesses to raise money by lottery for improving navigation on the Potomac River, helping Colonel Moore's 1769 draw, supporting another to help the Dismal Swamp Company import German workmen into North Carolina to finish a canal, and selling hundreds of the 10,000 tickets available at four dollars each for the 1784 Washington College lottery.

He also signed many tickets, which are now collector's items, for the Cumberland Mountain road scheme. This was designed to raise funds to build a road over the Allegheny Mountains to connect with Tidewater Virginia, where Washington had estate holdings. However, one cynical theory is that Washington only supported the scheme for the sake of his stepdaughter, twelve-year-old Patsy Curtis who suffered from epilepsy; the springs on the other side of the Allegheny Mountains to the west of Baltimore were thought to help alleviate the condition, but she could not travel over the primitive pack horse trails. A more likely explanation is that a mountain road was consistent with Washington's strategic vision that westward migration should drive the development of America. Whatever the truth, the lottery failed, as hardly any tickets were sold. He was not, however, automatically responsive. When Peregne Fitzhugh, son of a Maryland planter, family friend and one of his aides-de-camp in the Revolutionary War, held a lottery to avoid bankruptcy, he appealed to Washington to support it. Uncharacteristically, there is no evidence that his old commander ever bought any of the 3,827 ten-dollar tickets on offer.

When it was decided to build a capital city on the Potomac River, lotteries were called in aid, and Samuel Blodget, amateur architect and land speculator, was appointed to run them and oversee construction projects. The first, in 1793, was 'for improvement of the Federal City,' as Washington DC was then called, which offered a $50,000 hotel as top prize. The self-educated George Washington had long relied upon a young Harvard man, Tobias Lear, to run his office and paperwork. He had the highest regard and affection for this trusted lieutenant who was also charged with carrying out his final instructions to avoid being buried alive (a peculiar obsession of his) by ensuring his body was not put in a vault until at least two days after death. So he sent Lear a seven-dollar lottery ticket for his two-and-a-half-year-old son Benjamin, saying: 'if it should be his fortune to draw the Hotel it will add to the pleasure I feel in giving it.'

About 50,000 other tickets were sold, but the draw proceeded so slowly amid evidence that Blodget was conducting an unauthorised lottery for Georgia land that Washington, now in his second term as president, was forced to intervene. He warned that unless the errant agent behaved himself, he would expose him to the public. From then on, the draw went smoothly, with the grand hotel being won not by Benjamin Lear but Robert S. Bickley of Philadelphia. Unfortunately the hotel, due to be built on the northwest corner of Seventh and E streets, N.W. was never completed, and it took the luckless Bickley twenty years of legal action to claim its $50,000 value.

Meanwhile, another Blodget lottery, this time for new homes in the capital, also ran into trouble. The draw looked as if it would take ten years to complete, prompting the radical English journalist William Cobbett, then living in Philadelphia, to describe it in his *Porcupine's Gazette* as: 'a bait that cannot fail to catch the gulls …'. Other newspapers joined in and, faced with this early media frenzy, Blodget cancelled the scheme. It was not until 1812 that lotteries were again used to finance civic projects in the expanding new city, and then only if the president gave express permission.

Although Washington died a very wealthy man worth $530,000 net, excluding his land and slaves at the Mount Vernon estate, his haphazard attitude to money persisted until the end. Cash flow problems, caused by his assets being tied up in the 60,000 acres of land he owned from Ohio to New York, did not help and probably contributed psychologically to the curiously meticulous yet muddled way he ran his finances.

His complicated twenty-three-page will is revealing. Washington, who had no children, decided to leave some of his lottery winnings to his nephew, William Augustine Washington. These lots of lands in various Virginian townships are described in pedantic detail, yet it must have totally slipped his mind that only three years before drawing up this 1799 bequest he had already promised, in writing, the same prizes to another nephew, Bushrod Washington.

Appropriately, the Washington memorial, tribute to the great statesman, was built with the aid of a lottery. Plans for this prompted a British visitor, William Faux, to note in 1820 that he did not have a proper tomb and would not until 'a national grave is made up by lottery. Graves and Cathedrals are raised in this country, by means of lotteries!' But what was to prove the world's most notorious lottery was yet to come.

IF YOU REALLY WANT TO COMMIT ROBBERY, WHY NOT JUST START A LOTTERY?

17

LOUISIANA STATE LOTTERY

MOST CORRUPT EVER

Unlike Britain, lotteries in North America continued until well into the nineteenth century. They reached the zenith of their popularity between 1790 and 1860 when the finances of twenty-four of the thirty-three American states were greatly helped by draws which raised an estimated $32 million. That was how the west was really won.

The first authorised lottery in 1744 raised £7,500 to help protect the Massachusetts coast against the French. This was so successful that other colonies, including New York and Pennsylvania, soon imitated it. Lucky draws provided roads, defence, bridges, canals, schools and universities (Harvard, Yale, Brown, King's College now Columbia University) as well as many local projects including street lamps in Boston, paper mills in Philadelphia, clean drinking water for Baltimore, money to pay Indian land claims in New Jersey and vine-growing in California.

They even helped spread religion. More than 200 churches were erected with the proceeds; a lottery announcement for a church in Providence, Rhode Island, said the operators anticipated a rapid sale of tickets 'for the promulgation of the blessed Gospel of Peace.' With the exception of the Quakers, who from the start fiercely opposed lotteries on principle, all religious denominations benefited. As the *Columbian Centinel* put it in 1791: 'there is nothing in that sacred book [the Bible] which can be thought opposed to this method of gambling.'

They were readily accepted as a way of raising revenue for projects essential for building the new nation, particularly access into the interior, at a time when stock and bond issues were non-existent and there were only three incorporated banks. Then, as now, Americans were not fond of taxes. So, in the absence of an effective system of public credit, lotteries filled the breach. Under the headline 'PATRIOTISM OF THE LADIES', a news item of 28 April 1790 reported:

> When the Ladies [of Massachusetts] found the Government had established a Lottery to ease the taxes of the people, they generally became adventurers [lottery players] and it is pleasing to find that their Patriotism has been in some measure rewarded, by their sex sharing the FIRST CAPITAL PRIZE.

Over the following decades, however, attitudes changed as criminals exploited the game, as they had done in Britain. Lottery brokers operated all kinds of rackets and destroyed many lives, from labourers to businessmen; a teller in Washington's Mechanics' Bank lost $10,000 dollars and died destitute; a New York laboratory technician won $20,000 dollars, and squandered it all within twelve months; the owner of a profitable retail food chain lost $5,000 dollars, along with his business.

Social problems became so acute that on a bitterly cold January day in 1833 an abolitionist group addressed a huge meeting in the state capital, Philadelphia. Its spokesman, Job Roberts Tyson, read out a lengthy analysis of the 'evil tendencies' of the lottery system, which he denounced as an vicious British import; 5,000 copies were later printed and distributed throughout the US as a handbook for abolitionists. As in the mother country, the game caused suicides; on 2 January 1828 Oliver G. Kane, secretary of the National Marine Company, killed himself owing $140,000 and leaving a note saying his was the 'Tragedy of the Gamester.' Official statistics substantiate Tyson's catalogue of misery. Records of the Insolvent Court of Philadelphia for 1829–1833 show losses on lottery tickets by insolvent debtors ranging from $100 dollars (Joseph Brown) to a staggering $50,000 (the misnamed Thomas Hope).

Lottery mania worsened after 1825. Before then, there were only eight lottery dealers in New York, but by 1833 the number had soared to a total of 147. Complaints increased about advertisements disfiguring the main streets, already blighted by thousands of scavenging pigs and dogs, and touts thrusting handbills at passers-by. A local paper said visitors must think 'one half of the citizens get their living by affording the opportunity to gamble to the rest.' That was in 1827, the year most New York newspapers stopped accepting lottery advertisements. A British traveller, C.D. Arfwedson, described the lottery offices as 'numberless in Broadway. Their puffing exceeds all belief.' According to *The Lottery Exterminator*, published monthly by a public-spirited civil engineer J.A. Powers to expose frauds, there were more than 300 vendors in the city selling tickets on Sundays.

Despite the anti-lottery campaign, mismanagement of prizes, forgery of numbers, fraudulent numbers and non-payment of prizes spread to the fourteen legal lotteries operating in other US cities. The Civil War (1861–1865) helped slightly to revive the game as money was needed desperately, but thereafter fraud and abuse progressively led states, one by one, to drop it. There was one exception: the state of Louisiana. And it ran the most corrupt and controversial lottery ever played.

Critics who knock Camelot for taking 0.5 per cent of lottery revenues as profit might well reflect before crying 'too much' that the Louisiana State Lottery creamed off an amazing forty-eight per cent. Even by the standards of the time – in Italy, France and Austria all but fifteen per cent of the amount paid in was returned – this was clearly excessive.

Lawsuits, the militia, threats, blackmail and bribery were regular features of this lottery which ran continuously for twenty-five years from 1869, serviced by agents in every US city. At its peak, total sales per month from tickets sold from booths in bars, grocery stores, markets, laundries, on street corners, and outside churches, reached $2 million. The same amount was spent on advertising each year. Monthly prize money for tickets ranging from 50 cents to $40 amounted to $250,000 and twice yearly there was a top prize of $600,000 (about £6 million today). In addition to the lottery proper, there were two drawings daily whereby the poor of New Orleans lined up in long queues to spend their nickels and dimes at the booths in the hope of a dollar or two back.

The phenomenon threw up many eccentric characters: the forceful and persistent Anthony Comstock, agent for the New York Society for the Suppression of Vice who denounced the draw as 'a monstrous enterprise … conducted in open defiance of the law'; Alexander K. McClune, editor of the *Philadelphia Times*, who was sued for libel by the lottery company in a sensational case; and the Texan judge who announced from the bench during another lottery trial that the game was a good thing and pulled out of his pocket a ticket he had just bought.

The Louisiana saga started in 1866 when the foothold needed by a New York gambling syndicate, fronted by another colourful character, Charles T. Howard, was made easier by the state's carpetbag legislature. The syndicate was able to bribe it to pass a new Lottery Bill. Under this, the Louisiana Lottery Company, a private enterprise outfit which Howard controlled, would in return for a monopoly after 1869 pay the state $40,000 annually for twenty-five years, but be exempt from all other taxes. The directors named in the act were front men and Howard, who had previously worked for lotteries in Alabama and Kentucky, became president of the new company.

They began in 1869 with prizes of $1,264,000 in property, with the top prize being the St Louis Hotel. From then on the company, nicknamed the 'Octopus' because its tentacles spread from the Canadian border to Central America, spent huge sums in keeping out rivals and it controlled every Louisiana legislature until 1892. Only seven per cent of its revenues came from within the state itself; tickets were sold throughout the United States, the Caribbean and Mexico and, at one time, nearly half of all mail handled by the New Orleans Post Office was for lottery business. By 1890 shares in the company had soared to $1,200 compared to $35 in 1879, with the market value of the stock totalling more than double the whole of Louisiana's banking capital. Great care was taken to present an acceptable face. Howard even bought and converted Metaire Racecourse into a beautiful cemetery at a cost of $350,000, though some cynics alleged that, as an enthusiastic horse-racing fan, he only did so because the track's jockey club denied him membership.

The lottery did help the community, though. At its height in the 1880s it raised between $3 million and $5 million in net profit each year, which helped to build waterworks, cotton mills and sugar refineries .When New Orleans was devastated by floods in the spring of 1890, on a scale similar to Hurricane Katrina, it played a major role in raising money to pay for relief efforts. According to one eye witness, water rushed through 'with the speed of an express train' and ran for five miles, flooding all the streets and five thousand square miles of countryside beyond. Unlike the Katrina disaster, this time the Federal Government under President Benjamin Harrison's leadership reacted promptly to urgent pleas for help from Louisiana congressmen; within three hours both houses of Congress passed a money resolution to assist the stricken state. The lottery company sent $100,000 to State Governor Nicholls but he, aware that the operators were seeking a new charter from his legislature, sent it back, whereupon the company divided the amount among the various levee boards which needed funds for repairs. Another gift of $50,000, handed to Mayor Shakespeare of New Orleans, was accepted, though this provoked a spirited correspondence between the mayor and the Rev. Dr Corradine representing twelve Methodist churches who protested against the acceptance.

Throughout the 1880s, however, the company was constantly challenged in the courts for alleged malpractice, and legislators were accused of accepting bribes to vote in its favour. Some were virtually on its payroll. One, the Rev. N. W. Warren, said he needed money for a new roof for his church. Another, J. Fisher Smith, promised never to sell his vote however large the bribe might be. But when a lottery bill came before the Senate, he went into the 'Yes' lobby. Shortly afterwards he collapsed and died, and a money bag stuffed with $18,000 was found on his body. A few Louisiana politicians were not for sale. One fierce opponent, called McCann, was literally showered with money; he found banknotes under his hat each time he picked it up, banknotes under his plate at official dinners and banknotes floating from windows at his hotel. He always sent the money back.

The press attacked the lottery constantly; the *New Orleans Democrat* newspaper claimed if Methuselah had bought a daily ticket all his life, he would have spent about $250,000 to win $267,885. Gross profiteering by middlemen also stirred up public outrage. For a fee from the lottery organizers, they would take over the entire promotion, control and management of the game using brokers as their outlets. They were up to all kinds of tricks. During the 1880s in New Orleans, where you could bet on a particular number being drawn, trained parakeets would select, for a price, the number coming up next by squawking it out.

Despite the company being prepared to offer as much as $1 million for a twenty-five-year renewal of its franchise, the efforts of Comstock and his supporters began to succeed. The Anti-Lottery League of Louisiana was founded with its own newspaper, the *New Delta*, which put over robustly the abolitionist case. In 1890, the League held a conference at the Grunewald Opera House in New Orleans of almost 1,000 delegates from all over the state. Every single one was pledged to kill the lottery.

By that year – when forty-two out of the then forty-four states had banned lotteries – President Harrison agreed they were 'swindling and demoralizing agencies which debauched and defrauded' US citizens. He shut down the Louisiana draw by the very simple method of encouraging a bill denying it the use of mails. It was passed unanimously. As ninety-three per cent of lottery revenues came from outside the state, banning the interstate carriage of lottery tickets was a death blow. Prosaically but very effectively the federal postal authorities had won the day. And, in 1892, federal legislation was passed prohibiting the sale, drawing, advertising and soliciting of a lottery.

One of the last monthly public drawings of the Louisiana lottery was witnessed by Julian Ralph, correspondent for *Harpers Magazine*. This took place at 11am on a stage, set with a parlour scene and illuminated by gaslight, in a New Orleans theatre called the Academy of Music. Two white-haired former confederate generals smartly dressed in uniform, General Beauregard and Major-General Jubal A. Early acted as tellers. They were each paid $30,000 a year for their services. Beauregard, 'a fine, most gentlemanly-looking man,' stood by a silver lottery wheel with glass sides. Early, 'a perfect type of the conventional figure of Father Time,' stood by a very much larger wheel of multi-coloured boards. From the big wheel a blindfolded white boy took the numbers of the tickets, which Early read out. From the smaller wheel another blindfolded white boy selected domino-sized black envelopes containing the dollar prizes, which Beauregard read out. Two hundred tickets were drawn in this way and yielded very little. Suddenly, a major prize was won. 'Twenty eight thousand four hundred and thirty nine,' said Early; 'Three hundred thousand dollars,' said Beauregard.

'The effect was startling,' wrote Ralph:

Indeed, the startled senses refused to grasp the meaning of the words. The criers repeated the figures. The people in the theatre craned forward, a hundred pencils shot over pads or bits of papers in men's and women's laps. Then a murmur of voices sounded all over the house. The routine on the stage was halted, for the criers took the two bits of papers to some clerks, who sat at tables in the farther part of the stage, to allow them to verify the important figures. Then the routine began anew. The wheels were revolved every few minutes, and the rubber shells rattled around like coffee beans in a roasting-cylinder. The boys took off their bandages, and other boys were blindfolded and put in their places. The criers were relieved by others, and General Beauregard at last grew tired, and went out for half an hour. Among others came two criers who kept their hats on. Think of it! Their hats on, covered, in the presence of the God of Chance! It was an offence against the unities; it was making light of the solemn mystery of luck.

Foreshadowing the tactics of the United Kingdom's pirate radio operators of the 1960s, the lottery organizers did not give up easily, and they searched for a new sanctuary beyond North America, but with limited success. Even the queen of the Hawaiian Islands was approached but she refused to co-operate. What was left of the lottery moved eventually, in 1895, to Honduras where it became the Honduras National Lottery doing most of its business secretly in the US. Tickets printed at a clandestine printing office in Wilmington, Delaware, were carried around as the personal luggage of lottery employees using false names and the winning numbers were cabled to New Orleans in cipher. In June 1907, however, US Government agents raided the printing plant and closed down the ingenious draw. The biggest lottery scandal ever had finally come to an end. Lotteries were not to reappear in the US until the 1960s. Thirty years later they reappeared in the United Kingdom.

"HONEST JOHN"
BOOKIE

STRUCK
BY LIGHTNING
£50 / 3 million / 1

KILLED BY
TERRORISTS
6 million / 1

WINNING THE
LOTTERY
14 million / 1

IT COULD BE YOU, BUT...

18

IT NEVER COULD
BE YOU

Lotteries work to a pattern, their rhythm beating to social and economic forces. As the change from Regency to Victorian work ethic encouraged the ending, in 1826, of centuries of British lotteries, so too did the 'loadsa money' Thatcherite culture of the 1980s create the climate for their resurrection in the early 1990s.

Ironically, Margaret Thatcher herself opposed the rebirth. Her rejection, in February 1987, of a national lottery to help fund the National Health Service was undoubtedly due to her Methodist upbringing. 'I do not think,' she recalls in her Prime Ministerial memoirs, 'that the Government should encourage more gambling, let alone link it to people's health.'

It was left to her successor John Major, formerly PR for a bank, son of a circus acrobat and a considerable showman beneath his grey exterior, to sanction this rather risqué idea, then totally new to most people. But implementing such a bold and radical scheme to raise money for good causes through a harmless flutter, proved to be a rough, rollercoaster ride. Scandal, allegations of bribery, rows with the regulator, politicians and civil servants, all played out against a backdrop of razzmatazz, eerily echoed the past. The furore that greeted the announcement of Tory Prime Minister Harold Macmillan's premium bonds wheeze in 1956 should have warned enthusiasts that their path was not going to be smooth. The then shadow chancellor, Harold Wilson, spoke for many when he denounced the scheme as 'a squalid raffle', echoing the nineteenth-century critic who called the 1811 lottery 'a paltry way of raising supplies.'

But enough movers and shakers had seen how lotteries had funded the arts, sport, heritage and other good causes in Australia, where Tattersall's had been running them for 100 years, and also in Germany and Ireland, that the campaign for one in Britain, the only European country save Albania without, began to gain momentum.

When Major replaced Thatcher, they seized their chance and, following his unexpected election victory, on 18 December 1992 a bill to establish a national lottery was published by Peter Brooke, Minister in charge of the new Department of National Heritage. The media photographed him standing next to the old oak chest used to store paperwork in Neale's Million Lottery of 1694, an outstanding success as he hoped his would be. The legislation had three crucial provisions. Lottery money would be an addition to existing public spending and not a substitute for it. It would be privately run, in contrast to most other national lotteries which were, and continue to be, publicly owned. There would be one person, the director general of the Office of National Lottery (Oflot), to choose the consortium to run the lottery out of eight applicants and to regulate it thereafter. A former businessmen and accountant, Peter Davis took over this watchdog role. From the start, his work was met with a barrage of media criticism which, by temperament and background, he was ill-equipped to stem. One cartoon in *The Sun* cruelly showed the regulator at his desk while his secretary exclaims: 'Looks like it could be YOU Mr

Davis!', as the ubiquitous pointing finger brandishes a giant P45 outside the office window. Faced with the relentless criticism, Davis resigned in February 1998, but with his integrity intact, and a new regulator, the National Lottery Commission, replaced the one-man band of Oflot.

However, his choice of Camelot out of a strong field proved a shrewd move. The consortium was exceptionally well-qualified and experienced, and included the US gambling giant GTech, expert in gaming systems and technology software. This was run by Guy Snowden, a larger-than-life American entrepreneur who had grown the company from a tiny start-up in Rhode Island into a hugely profitable company which dominated the world lottery business. But Camelot still faced formidable competition. Virtually the entire British business establishment wanted to get in on the act including a late entrant, the People's Lottery, a bid by Richard Branson who envisaged the game being run as a charitable foundation.

As has happened since the seventeenth century with rival lottery operators, accusations of dirty tricks flew fast and furious. Anonymous brown envelopes containing lurid accusations of GTech's dubious business methods were sent to business journalists, and Branson complained that Snowden had tried to bribe him to withdraw his bid. Amid intense media and political interest, Davis announced Camelot the victor on the grounds it was most likely to maximize ticket sales for good causes.

The triumphant consortium was smart enough to learn the lessons of the New Hampshire sweepstakes lottery of 1964, first in the US for seven decades, which failed dismally. And it failed for the very simple reason that it was so boring. The draw was held every six months, there was no excitement and the top prizes were measured in just thousands of dollars. This flouted an age-old principle: 'What lottery providers have known for centuries,' said Alan Greenspan, former Federal Reserve chairman, 'is that people pay more for a claim on a very big pay-off, and that's where the profits from lotteries have always come from.'

So, as a deliberate policy, Camelot offered big prizes and invested huge amounts in promotion to drum up ticket sales. This brash marketing approach worked. Big prizes always mean big sales; a million lottery tickets were being sold per hour in London in October 2006 when £74 million was available in Camelot's main draw and its EuroMillions draw. Its 1994 publicity campaign cost £40 million and featured the famous 'It Could Be You' adverts. They were seen on average thirteen times by forty million adults and sold some £46 million worth of tickets for the first draw which took place, amid huge hype, on Saturday 19 November 1994 – Britain's most intense national event since VE Day. Everyone wanted to play, from the prime minister to office clerks clubbing together, just as maids in aristocratic houses had done in Neale's 1693 lottery. In the first rollover 96 per cent of the adult population bought a ticket. The lottery quickly became a national institution and an integral part of everyday life.

Despite the honest but ill-advised confession of Camelot CEO Dianne Thompson that odds of 1 in 14 million for the jackpot are so great that it is almost certainly never going to be you, the British lottery continues to be one of the most successful in the world. (To be fair, the overall odds of winning a prize in the main draw are 1 in 54, and 1 in 24 for the EuroMillions draw.) Jeremiahs predicted the game would fail miserably to fund good causes; the reverse was true. It has raised more than £22 billion for good causes, created tens of thousands of new jobs, funded 250,000 local projects, made 2,200 millionaires or multi-millionaires, pays out four million prizes a week and is played by two out of three UK adults, including the Queen. She once won a £10 prize, prompting the inevitable headline 'ONE'S WON'. In a tradition dating back centuries, it has made possible flagship projects, some of them controversial, including Tate Modern (£57.7 million of lottery cash), renovation of the Royal Opera House (£75.5 million), the new Wembley Stadium (£120 million), the Eden Project in Cornwall (£53 million), the Millennium Dome (£628 million) and the 2012 London Olympics (£2.2 billion).

The British lottery's first multi-millionaire was Mukhtar Mohidin, an Asian factory worker from Blackburn in the Midlands, who won £17.8 million. But this 'good fortune' led to vicious rows among his extended and close-knit family who fell out among themselves over the amounts he generously gave them. He was followed by Jackie King, whose £14 million win in 1998 wrecked her marriage, Michael Carroll, a young Norfolk dustman and tearaway who won £9.7 million only to squander most of it by 2007, and others. Although their spectacular misfortunes have grabbed the headlines, they paint a distorted picture. Two in three winners return to work, and ninety-six per cent say they are happier since the win. Some are even philosophical about blowing their fortune. One of the first of the lottery millionaires, Michael Antonucci, went on a twelve-year spending spree after borrowing £10 from his mother to buy tickets which won him £2.8 million. He spent the lot on failed business ventures, luxury cars and having a good time. Back in his old job exporting antique furniture to the US, he said: 'you don't want to die as the richest man in the graveyard.'

The most controversial Camelot winner was Iorworth Hoare, a jailed rapist from Leeds. When he won £7 million in 2004, a third of a £21 million lottery prize, there was national outcry. Hoare, son of a coal miner and then aged fifty-two, was staying at a Middlesbrough bail hostel, on weekend leave from Leyhill open prison in Gloucestershire, when he bought his lucky ticket. He immediately began splashing out and boasting: 'I'm made for life now.' As his fortune was about to earn him nearly £7,000 a week interest during the remainder of his jail term, this was certainly true. But within hours of hitting the jackpot with numbers 3, 5, 8, 18, 28 and 48, he was picked up by police and locked up in a high security jail with future weekend leave cancelled, apparently in case he decided to use his money to abscond, but 'in reality,' remarked one commentator, 'because his win made the rest of us as mad as hell.'

Government Ministers tried to deprive him of his windfall on the grounds that he was a serial sex offender and did not, therefore, 'deserve' his win. They forgot that anyone, good or bad, can win the lottery; that's the whole point of it. Its very randomness makes it blind to both vice and virtue, and some winners share their good fortune. Sheffield pensioners Ray and Barbara Wragg have given £5.5 million of the £7.6 million they won in 2000 to charity and friends. Others simply do not claim their good fortune. In August 2002, *The Sun* newspaper, under the headline 'Who's the dozy lad walking around with £1 million winning card?' reported:

> A dozy youth is sitting on a fortune with a £1 MILLION-winning Lotto scratchcard stuffed in the back pocket of his jeans.
>
> The lad went into a newsagents thinking he had won £2 on the Cash For Life Game but stunned staff told him he'd actually scooped £2,000 a month for LIFE.
>
> Incredibly, he was too busy worrying about missing a bus to take in the bombshell. He hurriedly paid for a magazine, and then dashed out to catch it. He has not been back.

Although there are 180 days to claim a prize, as of March 2007 a total of £900 million, including jackpots of £1 million and £2 million, had not been claimed – three per cent of total prizes paid out at £30 billion. The unclaimed money always goes to good causes.

Drama was not confined to the players. Snowden resigned after losing a libel action brought by Branson over the alleged bribe attempt, said to have taken place over lunch at the Virgin chief's home in Holland Park. The case also contributed to Davis's resignation when it re-emerged in court that he had naively accepted a lift in a GTech corporate jet a few months after awarding the licence to Camelot.

Early on there were accusations that Camelot, dubbed 'Scamelot' by the satirical magazine *Private Eye*, dished out contracts exclusively to its own shareholders without putting the contracts out to tender. 'Fat cat' scandals with directors pocketing huge bonuses in 1997 whipped up another media storm.

Sensibly, Camelot switched its advertising stance from the 'It Could Be You' greed to the benefit of good causes. Another battle was to keep the distribution of lottery funding at arm's length from politicians following the 2002 uproar over grants given to controversial groups. Middle England was outraged that the lottery funded politically correct projects while ex-servicemen and other worthy causes appeared to be left out. Cash for a lesbian, gay and bisexual pantomime in Manchester, a newsletter for deaf homosexuals in Birmingham, help for isolated Chinese women in Gloucestershire and for old people denied their rights in the Ukraine, an advice centre for Scottish prostitutes, and a new 'focal point' for bilingual Welsh farm-workers were among the projects that fanned the flames of indignation. More than 100,000 people supported a ferocious campaign by the *Daily Mail* for direct government control on where the proceeds went; only swift sleight of hand by the Department of Culture, Media and Sport (DCMS) in rejigging the funding bodies prevented this.

A second Branson attempt to win the lottery licence was beaten off by Camelot Chief Executive Dianne Thompson, a no-nonsense Yorkshirewoman just five feet tall who claimed to have 'balls of steel'. In 2000, he appeared to have won the shambolic contest for the second seven-year licence after the National Lottery Commission announced it would negotiate solely with his not-for-profit People's Lottery bid. The process descended into farce when the feisty Thompson had that decision overturned in court and went on to win. It was she, too, who halted the slump in ticket sales caused by natural 'player fatigue' that so worried the Government in 2003 that it hinted it might need to nationalise the game. By then nearly 200 terminals had been removed after failing to hit Camelot's minimum weekly sales targets, causing *Retail Express*, newspaper of the UK's news retailers, to label the company 'National Floppery'.

The launch of scratchcards, new games played via mobile phones and the internet, midweek as well as weekend draws, and EuroMillions linked to equivalent games in Europe, paying out jackpots of £100 million plus, gradually pushed up overall sales again. In August 2007, the EuroMillions game rolled over three times to offer a £35.4 million top prize. This was won by Glasgow postal worker Angela Kelly, making her Britain's biggest lottery winner and richer than Princes William and Harry. The odds of scooping such a jackpot are, however, 1 in 76 million – the same as John Prescott's chances of winning the 100 metres at the 2012 Olympics, according to bookmaker William Hill.

Initially, a battle royal looked likely for the third licence to run the National Lottery after the Government announced it could last for fifteen years from February 2009 – more than double its original length. Confident predictions were made of a whole galaxy of bidders playing to win one of the biggest prizes in the business world. Despite claims it had failed to meet its own targets for good causes, Camelot remained firm favourite on the basis of an impressive track record, formidable knowledge of lottery playing trends, a tried and tested CEO, and essential technological support from its partners ICM and GTech. It also held a trump card: fear of the game falling into the hands of an unknown operator when it was committed to raising so much for the 2012 Olympics.

One by one, potential competitors dropped out as they realised the odds they faced: 'About the same as a punter winning the jackpot,' said one wag. The prohibitive cost of bidding also deterred them. 'I'm not going to throw away another £10m and waste an enormous amount of work and effort if the dice are stacked against me,' declared Branson as he withdrew from the race. When the deadline for bids closed on Friday 9 February 2007, only two companies entered the lists; Camelot and India's largest lottery company, Sugal and Damani, which for thirty-five years had run the game in four Indian states, handling twenty-five million transactions a day. The two contenders needed to get past seven hurdles, including financial probity, technological capability, business plan and, crucially, credible ideas for raising money for good causes. The Mumbai-based privately-owned conglomerate, which owns hotels, stock broking firms, jewellery stores and diamond concerns, put up a cost-effective bid based on using its own innovative software. But there was never any doubt, in the minds of most observers, that in this particular David and Goliath contest the giant – with its five million word bid, weighing a massive 202 kilograms and produced at the cost of £20 million – would emerge the winner. So no-one was surprised when on 7 August 2007 the National Lottery Commission announced that Camelot was three times lucky on the grounds it would probably sell the most tickets, bringing in £22 billion for good causes over ten years.

There is an option to extend the third licence, increased from seven years to ten, for another five years. If Camelot, a private company owned equally by five diverse shareholders – Cadbury Schweppes, Royal Mail Enterprises, De La Rue Holdings, Fujitsu Services and Thales Electronics – wins the extension, it will have managed the draw for nearly thirty years. By then, in 2024, the lottery world will be as different as the modern game now is from a church raffle circa 1935.

I'D LIKE MY LOTTERY MONEY TO GO
TO GAMBLERS ANONYMOUS, PLEASE

19

DOES THE FUTURE BELONG TO BIG BROTHER?

Tick-boxes on tickets allowing buyers to choose charities; using the tickets for weekly plebiscites on current issues; a brain-scan service that measures consumer response to lottery commercials; satellite navigation to guide you to the nearest lottery retailer; lotteries as part of the burgeoning virtual gaming industry; and a world lottery with £500 million jackpots. All are feasible due to increasingly sophisticated technology.

Fears are increasing, however, that technological advances, now accelerating at an unimagined rate, are bringing nearer the society of George Orwell's prophetic novel *Nineteen Eighty-Four* where thoughts are read and controlled. Or, less alarming but still disturbing, the society of Aldous Huxley's 1932 *Brave New World*, in which technology has taken control. What is certain is that lotteries will become part of the twenty-four-hour interactive (possibly total surveillance) society where everyone is connected to everyone else and monitored via the ever-widening range of communication devices spawned by the information technology revolution.

Already, it is technically possible for ticket buyers to vote for which good cause they would prefer their money to support. Since computerised betting systems can record the numbers selected, it may also be possible to use the ticket to tick your choice of charities. Naturally this could not be binding on the Department of Culture, Media and Sport (DCMS), which is responsible for the National Lottery, but it would be a handy rough guide to the preferences of the seven in ten who play. At the same time, it would help to involve them in the way the money is spent, thus contributing to the democratic process.

In October 2002, the DCMS eventually accepted this radical idea to put tick-boxes on cards, giving purchasers a choice of charities, and said it would give people 'more say about giving money locally and for causes they want.' Camelot, though warning that the necessary software changes would be costly, announced it was happy to discuss the idea with the regulators. However the Community Fund, one of the five bodies then distributing lottery money, was unenthusiastic, welcoming 'more public involvement' in lottery funding decisions but claiming the box-ticking plan was not the right way. That was also the view of the National Council of Voluntary Organisations when the idea was revived three years later, with plans for television game shows asking viewers to vote on which are the most deserving causes. Giving the public a voice on the money was thought to be a neat and effective way of maintaining confidence in the game. But charities were alarmed at the thought of a television programme in which celebrities competed to put the case for individual grant applications. The council warned this was a crude approach, benefiting populist causes at the expense of smaller and less high-profile organizations. However, in 2007, the sustainable transport charity, Sustrans, won a £50 million lottery grant, the 'People's Millions' prize, through the public voting on a TV show. The experiment was rated a success. So far practical problems have delayed tick-boxes for worthy causes, which would also need Parliamentary approval, but if the technicalities could be sorted then it is possible to go further still.

Why not use the lottery ticket as a weekly plebiscite on issues of the day? Employ the betting system to produce a snapshot of public opinion, a kind of mass observation technique for the twenty-first century? A simple multi-choice question printed on the ticket could, for example, ask: 'Are you in favour of public spending on the arts staying the same, less or more?' Although less accurate than modern market research methods, it could be a useful steer on contemporary issues. One danger is the possibility of a future unscrupulous government hijacking such a system, bypassing Parliament and ruling by popular decree. A bit fanciful perhaps, but not entirely impossible.

Orwellian techniques are certainly creeping in. Camelot, which has a staggering annual marketing budget of £70 million, has already used Pre-Diction. Developed by Professor Richard Silberstein, an Australian neuroscientist when researching Alzheimer's disease, this is a service that allows advertisers to research how people will react to their campaigns by measuring the brain's response to a commercial. It relies on sensors in headsets to measure electrical activity in the brain which is then relayed to an advanced software system. Camelot used it to test an ad featuring Billy Connolly, although only after it appeared on TV. While this technique cannot read the minds of consumers it can identify a positive or negative response and measure how strong it is. Who can rule out the possibility that advances in the field of neuro-psychology will eventually result in the ability of advertisers, lottery organisers and, most worryingly, governments to gain access to what people are thinking?

The idea of a world lottery is not new. It has been around since the early 1970s. Initially, it was proposed as an annual draw run by the United Nations, but licensed by the government of each participating country. In 2003, a detailed scheme for both a global lottery and a global premium bond to raise money for development finance worldwide was published by the UN University. This argued for a single global lottery sold worldwide and run by one organization. There would be an agreed international framework to regulate the lottery organizers, transfer the money into a central fund run by the UN, and distribute it to worthy development projects round the globe. But, given the impossibility of persuading so many governments to agree and implement such a complex scheme, it was always going to be commercial interests that did it.

Hence Camelot's imaginative plan, part of its successful third licence bid, for the first ever world lottery draw. Together with fifty of the biggest national lotteries in Europe, Australia and the Far East and state lotteries in the US, it proposes a worldwide draw creating more than 100 millionaires a month. The monthly game will build up to an annual prize of up to £500 million drawn during a key holiday season or event for maximum sales impact. Individual numbered balls are to be picked in every continent across different time zones and broadcast during a live television show when, as a dramatic climax, a final ball is selected completing the winning number sequence.

For other glimpses of the future, there is Brazil where the lottery network is used to pay utility bills and pay benefits, and India where paying your electricity bill as you play the lottery is normal. Sugal and Damani, the Indian lottery operator and the only company to challenge Camelot for the third lottery licence, also run a lottery rickshaw. Three-wheeler cycles pedal around with terminals linked by wireless to the lottery computers; similar terminals in the back of London black cabs cannot be far off.

By 2009 more than 4.5 million people in the UK had registered to play lottery games on the internet, interactive TV and their mobile phones. Buying tickets by remote control in this way might well increase the chances of lottery addiction. At present this is not generally seen as a problem even by the harshest critics, save for teenagers over-indulging in 'Instant Scratchcard' lotto games. But the sheer ease of carrying out a transaction by mobile phone or other mobile device must encourage addictive personalities to play to excess. Camelot, along with the communications company Orange, broadcaster BSkyB, online marketplace eBay and ticket sales giant Ticketmaster, plans new ways of playing through interactive platforms. It will also expand the system which enables you to pay for tickets at checkouts with the groceries. More than 100,000 points of sale are promised by 2013. In the age of reality TV, the company is also developing online 'lifestyle' games for young adults which offer prizes such as a night out with their favourite celebrity. Non-cash prizes for other games may include house makeovers.

Nor is it neglecting the astonishing growth of virtual gaming – the three-dimensional spaces on the internet where you can create and play with your own on-screen characters called 'avatars'. Hundreds of millions of people worldwide will inhabit this parallel universe by 2010 and, in anticipation, Camelot is well through the electronic looking-glass with plans for multi-player interactive games. These may include elements of both chance and skill, such as a motor racing game or Sudoku.

Whether Camelot can sustain sales over the next decade must be doubtful. History shows that people grow bored and stop playing as time passes, whatever novelties and incentives are introduced.

Despite Gordon Brown's subtle curbing of New Labour's curious obsession with the gaming industry, Camelot also faces competition from the deregulation of the gaming laws. Even before this came into effect in September 2007, online gaming, available seven days a week, twenty-four hours a day, 365 days a year, had become Britain's new craze; a million people regularly place bets via the internet, staking an average of £1,000 each year. At the same time, new casinos were permitted able, for the first time, to lure punters in with glossy promotions and cheap booze. The country's 8,500 bookies were also allowed to install a total of 30,000 fruit machines in their high street offices, with poker and blackjack machines to follow. All this at a time when a typical

British family spends £3.60 each week on gambling, 80p more than it spends on fruit.

Some academics blame the state-led gambling explosion – with £50 billion spent in 2006, a sevenfold increase in just five years – on the resurrection of the National Lottery, which made betting respectable. More likely it is simply the symptom of a national characteristic, not its cause, since lotteries and gambling have been linked for centuries; the lotteries preceding the South Sea Bubble were also blamed for preparing the ground for that disaster.

What is certain is that technology, which ought to be a means to an end, is fast becoming an end in itself. Is it too fanciful to imagine that ever more sophisticated media techniques, and ever tighter regulation of human behaviour, will increase social control and robotic responses to the point that the dream of human freedom turns into a totalitarian nightmare? Or can systems of random selection help the democratic process?

ARISE, SIR 1-14-22-27-36-41....

20

CRACKPOTS OR VISIONARIES?

'There would never be a fair lottery.' So wrote the Scottish political economist and philosopher Adam Smith in his 1776 ground-breaking treatise *The Wealth of Nations*. But was he right? And could the underlying principle of randomness be extended beyond financial lotteries?

From Ancient Greece to Renaissance Italy, societies have drawn lots to ensure that no-one holds office long enough to be corrupted and to throttle self-serving bureaucracies and fossilised hierarchies. In Britain, the last serious proposal to govern by lottery appeared in 1659, among a raft of radical constitutions drawn up between Cromwell's death and the restoration of the monarchy. 'At this time the Opinions of Men were much divided concerning a Form of Government', say the memoirs of Edmund Ludlow MP, army officer and signatory to Charles I's death warrant. He outlined the various schemes which ranged widely from selection by the contemporary Great and Good, to democratic elections and a system remarkably similar to our House of Commons and House of Lords. There were also various ideas based on the perpetual rotation of elected representatives, including a 1,000-strong law-making body, with a third being replaced each year through, it is implied, random selection.

The Victorian historian Macaulay summed up these proposals as 'hereditary senates, senates appointed by lot, annual senates, [and] perpetual senates.' Dryly, he added:

> In these plans nothing was omitted … Polemarchs and Phylarchs, Tribes and Galaxies, the Lord Archon and the Lord Strategus. Which ballot boxes were to be green and which red, which balls were to be of gold and which of silver.

Not everyone was impressed by the torrent of constitutions; one satire published late in 1659 proposed an expedition 'to Survey the Government of the Moon … as Lunaticks.' Nevertheless, the idea of a classic republican commonwealth in which all citizens would participate was forcefully promoted, particularly by a neglected radical, soldier, pamphleteer and publisher called John Streater. He took as his model an Adriatic Free State of 30,000 people which, centuries ahead of its time, introduced a universal medical service in 1301, old people's homes in 1347 and abolished slave trading in 1418. This was the republic of Ragusa, situated on the southernmost coast of present-day Croatia, and now better known as the over-crowded tourist destination of Dubrovnik. The parallels between this remarkably liberal state and the Ancient Greeks are striking. The head of state served for just a month at a time before being replaced; the sixty-member senate, the supreme governing body, sat for one year only in order to prevent any one family from dominating; and all aristocratic males sat, compulsorily, on the grand council, the executive body, from the age of eighteen. Civil servants were routinely rotated through a complicated system of random selection involving the plucking of gold balls, iron balls, and linen balls from an urn. 'By this often changing of Officers, they preserve themselves,' claimed Streater in his treatise, *Government Described*.

A century later the mandatory rotation of office holding became a cardinal tenet of early American republicanism, the omission of this principle in the federal constitution sparking off widespread protest from US President and founding father, Thomas Jefferson downwards. The constitution, however, still amazed the conservative world, particularly China. 'These barbarians have no monarch whatsoever,' wrote a Chinese official to his emperor in 1800. 'The tribe have several headmen who are selected by the drawing of lots for terms of four years apiece.'

Even though the mechanics of the regular lottery for running ancient Dubrovnik were complex and minutely regulated, the idea was simple. It was to stop corruption and make government truly collective by rendering it impossible for any individual to abuse his power or exercise undue influence. Or, as another English radical, Gerrard Winstanley, who preached a kind of primitive communism, put it at the time: 'If water stand long, it corrupts; whereas running water keeps sweet.' Streater concedes England had never been such a free state, but adds hopefully that it could be 'if the Legislators can hit upon the Mark of denying themselves in perpetuating their Power.' Some hope. It was to be another 340 years before the idea of using random selection in the political process began, tentatively, to re-emerge in late-1990s Britain.

On the surface, a political lottery looks like an anarchist dream come true. Yet it prevents the abuse of power by redistributing it regularly and is a fair way of selection. For 2,000 years, writers and thinkers have fiercely debated its merits. In *The Republic*, Plato argued for a mating lottery which would allocate sexual partners at the time of marriage festivals. There would certainly be downsides and upsides to that!

In Thomas More's *Utopia*, town houses are reallocated every ten years by lot, while 'anyone who deliberately tries to get himself elected to a public office [in Utopia] is permanently excluded from holding one.' In *The Social Contract*, the French philosopher Jean-Jacques Rousseau urges the random selection of legislators. The Enlightenment thinker Montesquieu agreed, and argued, 'the suffrage by lot is natural to democracy as that by choice is to aristocracy.' Other intellectuals have been opposed, notably the political theorist Edmund Burke. In his famous 1790 essay *Reflections on the Revolution in France*, he wrote: 'No rotation; no appointment by lot; no mode of election operating in the spirit of sortition or rotation can be generally good in a government conversant in extensive subjects.' Yet now, in the twenty-first century, the case is re-emerging for achieving social justice and equality by distributing power, money, jobs, goods houses and education through regular and random reallocation.

Realistically, vested interests would move to kill such a revolutionary approach if it looked to be winning any significant support. And yet it is blinkered to dismiss out of hand the basic premise. The former Greater London Council used to organise small-scale housing lotteries. Artist Alan Rossiter won a house in a lottery in 1977 for £1. It was in Albion Road in Hackney, east London and for three years he did not have to pay anything. He then paid £9,300 for it, and was amazed to discover in 2007 that it was worth £800,000. For years in the United States sophisticated housing lotteries have helped allocate affordable homes for the less well-off. In Massachusetts, under state legislation known as the 'anti-snob' zoning act, there is a scheme to construct such homes, using locally granted permits allowing the developer to build at a higher density than normal. Private developers work with local authorities to create the estates, selling the units at a set price to first-time buyers with incomes at or below eighty per cent of the average income for the area. Preference is given to applicants who are residents of the community, parents with children still living with them, and municipal employees such as firemen, policemen or teachers. Names of successful applicants are then drawn randomly at the local town hall or shopping mall and placed in order of drawing. For social reasons again, many US universities use lotteries to allocate rooms to students rather than renting them to those who can afford them. And in Brazil, Sao Paulo has a housing lottery just for single women.

Education is another area. After weeks of debate, on 27 February 2007, Brighton and Hove City Council voted to become the first local authority in Britain to allocate places in its most popular, over-subscribed schools by lottery. Previously, priority in the city had been given to those who lived closest to schools. Now there are six catchment areas and pupils are expected to go to a school in their area. But where there are two schools in one catchment area, admissions are decided by computer-generated random selection and not by proximity.

This bold move by the Labour-run authority instantly sparked off a nationwide debate. Newspaper columnists had a field day. *The Daily Mail*'s rumbustious Keith Waterhouse wrote:

> Having by this time got the whole country into a gambling tizz, there is no reason why it should stop at our children's future. What about hospital waiting lists? Why wait six months for your operation when, at the spin of a wheel or the turn of a card, you can reduce it to six days. Need a council house? Try the Lottery. A clutch of homes going every week in the exciting new National Lottery game. Housey-housey.

Yet it is a selection method which is commonplace in education elsewhere in the world. 'This is not a wacky idea that has come out of nowhere,' said the then Schools Minister Andrew Adonis of the controversial new Admissions Code, due to apply to pupils starting secondary school in September 2008. This allows councils to allocate places randomly where schools are over-subscribed. Some right-wing commentators disagreed, one even harrumphing that the innovation marked 'a painful moment in our national decline and fall.' Councils from Norfolk to Dorset debated whether to follow suit as supporters argued random selection was fairer, promoted equality and diversity and stopped popular schools becoming the preserve of affluent parents who could afford to buy houses nearby. Opponents, meanwhile, organised a ferocious campaign to stop the lottery system being introduced nationally, denouncing it as a frightening experiment in social engineering, which threatened to sink the house values of Middle England.

Jurors are chosen at random. Virtually everyone, with the possible exception of the Government, seems to want to keep this well-tried and tested system, which has been around since the time of Magna Carta. Some want it extended to help decide public policy through the idea of voters being randomly selected for citizens' jury service. This would require everyone over the age of eighteen to debate and pass judgment on health, education and the criminal justice system at least twice in their adult lives. These juries are already widely used on a voluntary basis in Australia, Germany, Spain, India and the United States and there have been several interesting experiments in the UK. Within days of becoming Prime Minister, Gordon Brown took the first faltering step toward setting up such a service, but has so far shrunk from making it compulsory, which enthusiasts say is crucial to its success.

In the Second World War the Bevin Boys – named after the wartime labour minister Ernest Bevin – were chosen at random to mine coal as part of the war effort. So many regular miners had been conscripted to fight that coal reserves, essential for defeating Hitler, had fallen dangerously. From 1943 to 1948 more than 47,000 young men were called up to take their place, one in ten of all conscripts. A lottery decided whether they were sent to the forces or the pits. The process in those pre-computer days was unsophisticated, but apparently accepted as fair which was important since the Bevin Boys, being out of uniform, were sometimes accused of cowardice or desertion. Every month for twenty months, one of Bevin's secretaries simply pulled a number from a hat, and all men whose draft number ended in that digit went to the coal face.

During a unique initiative in 2003, the Canadian province of British Columbia randomly selected a group of 160 citizens to form a Citizens' Assembly on Electoral Reform. Their job was to propose a new electoral system for the provincial government.

Letters of invitation were sent to 15,800 British Columbians whose names were picked at random, by computer, from the BC voters' list. The idea was to reflect the gender, age and geographical make-up of the electorate by this initial step. Names of those to serve were then drawn at random from a hat at public meetings through the province in what was hailed as an historic experiment.

Darleen Dixon, a sixty-five-year-old fabric store owner and retired nursing administrator, was the first member selected, followed by a sevety-one-year-old rancher Wilt Chelle. 'It really is Power to the People', said an excited Jack Blaney, chair of the assembly at the Fort St George draw. News media and the public were initially sceptical and condescending about the ability of laymen to deal with the complexities, but that soon changed as Darleen and the group set to work. Only one member withdrew during a hard eleven-month slog studying alternative electoral systems with the help of specialist advisers. The assorted ranchers, retired nurses, teachers and lorry drivers were genuinely independent and non-partisan, and they did a difficult job well. They proved that a group of laymen is quite capable of dealing rationally with complex political issues. The assembly recommended replacing the 'First Past the Post' electoral system with a single transferable vote scheme. On 17 May 2005, this was put to the electorate in a referendum which required a sixty per cent approval. Although it narrowly failed to achieve this with 57.7 per cent in favour, British Columbia can justly claim to have fashioned a new democratic tool which has since been used in Ontario, South Australia and elsewhere.

A British citizens' assembly was debated in the House of Commons in June 2006 when Labour backbencher David Chaytor presented his Parliamentary and Local Elections (Choice of Electoral System) Bill. This would have allowed randomly selected voters to consider different voting systems for parliamentary and local elections and make recommendations for decision by a national referendum. Although opponents dismissed the idea as 'an adventure playground for political anoraks', a surprisingly large number of MPs voted for it. The Bill was, however, rejected by 168 votes to 72, a majority of 94 against.

In the United States, lotteries have selected conscripts to fight in wars that include World War One, World War Two and Vietnam. Making military service subject to chance was not always popular. 'It puts the solemn obligation to serve one's country on a par with the Las Vegas gaming tables', complained one senator of the 1970 military draft. There were also strong complaints that this draw was biased, on account of the numbers being insufficiently mixed.

However, the lottery that would be used today to send young men to Iraq and Afghanistan, in the event of president and Congress approving such a drastic move, is claimed to be the most equitable in history. Elaborate plans have already been drawn up by a federal agency called the Selective Service System (SIS), which is independent of the Defence Department: all males aged between eighteen and twenty-five and living in the US must, by law, register with it. There are crucial differences from the Vietnam draft lottery whose logistics led up to seven years' uncertainty for some conscripts and allowed others, most famously President Clinton, to escape military service if they could prove they were full-time students.

Under this new lottery, a man would spend only one year in the first priority for the draft – either the calendar year he turns twenty or the year his deferment ends. If he is not drafted in his first priority year, he drops into second priority. Each year after that, he is placed in an increasingly lower priority group and his liability for the draft lessens accordingly. This spares him the frustration of waiting until his twenty-sixth birthday to be certain he is not drafted. At the same time a college student will have his call-up postponed only until the end of the current academic year, thus stopping the abuse of continuing in college and being deferred from service until too old to be conscripted.

This scheme is designed to work on a principle remarkably like that used in the draws from the two 'wheels' that took place at London's Guildhall in the eighteenth century. The US National Institute of Standards and Technology (NIST) has developed a unique calendar and number selection scheme whereby each day of the year is selected randomly by computer and placed in a capsule. Numbers from one to 365 (366 for men born in leap year) are also selected randomly and placed in capsules which are then placed in a second drum. At the draw, to be broadcast on coast-to-coast television under the scrutiny of observers, officials and media, one capsule is drawn from the birth dates drum and one capsule from the sequenced numbers drum. They are matched to decide the order of the call-up.

For example, if 23 July is drawn first from the 'date' drum and number 30 is drawn simultaneously from the 'numbers' drum, those turning twenty on 23 July will be drafted only after men whose birthdays drew sequence numbers one to twenty-nine. The drawings continue until all 365 (or 366) birthdays of the year are paired with sequence numbers.

This is a far cry from the first US military lottery, used to raise Union Army forces during the American Civil War. Then, the rich could escape by paying a fee of $300 to be excused from service. As the newspapers printed the names of those drafted and their occupations, it swiftly became obvious that only working-class men were being drawn. As a result, on 13 July 1863, outside the New York lottery headquarters building, a mob of thousands gathered hurling bricks and granite paving stones through the windows and then setting fire to it. Shortly, two city blocks were ablaze, soldiers fired on the crowd but were forced to retreat and it took them three days to bring the city under control. The final total of the most serious riot in US history was more than 100 dead, 3,000 homeless, and $1.5 million in property damage. 'The Civil War in America is at an end. Who would have looked forward to civil war in New York?' asked *The Times*.

The US also has a lottery for would-be immigrants from certain countries. Every year this gives 50,000 people Green Cards, to live and work permanently there. Hopefuls from Afghanistan to Zimbabwe register online for the annual draw, paying an application fee of $34.50 for a single application and $59 for a family application. There are some educational and immigration requirements. Countries with high numbers of immigrants already entering the US, including Canada, the United Kingdom, China, India and Russia, are excluded. If they are awarded a coveted Green Card, the fortunate winners also receive free airline tickets to the US. Each year, more than ten million people try their luck since the odds, roughly 1 in 150, are immeasurably better than those of any financial lottery.

The US also uses lotteries to decide which prospectors will be permitted to lease government lands with oil and gas reserves. This harks back to an older tradition when land lotteries were common such as the Georgia land draws of the 1830s and the 1901 federal lottery that distributed homesteads in Oklahoma. In 1826 the property of Thomas Jefferson, third president of the United States and main author of the Declaration of Independence, was distributed by lottery.

The lottery is traditionally used in extreme conditions. In 1985, in two Brazilian prisons at Belo Horizonte an ingenious 'lottery of death' was held. Prisoners launched a most effective protest against appalling living conditions and overcrowding by selecting some fellow-prisoners by lot and killing them. The publicity so stoked public anger that the Brazilian Government was forced to alleviate the overcrowding with a special grant of US $60 million. In 2008, Burma distributed food by lottery in the aftermath of Cyclone Nargis, the worst natural disaster in its history.

In Britain, demand is growing for radical change in the political system at a time when the nation has the fewest elected representatives per 1,000 votes anywhere in Europe. Disenchantment is at an all-time high. The 2005 general election returned New Labour with a healthy 66 majority, but with the active support of barely one in five of the total of those eligible to vote – the lowest share of the vote for any governing party since 1918 and lowest in the European Union, bar Estonia and Lithuania. Twelve months later a survey found that only one in four believed politicians told the truth. Another poll, for the Committee for Parliamentary Standards, suggested the public puts MPs below estate agents in terms of trustworthiness. No wonder some reformers – visionaries or crackpots, depending on your point of view – believe only a truly radical change can engage voters.

'More than any other political group the Lords is a body chosen by lot.' So said Lord Cranborne, the then Tory leader in the House of Lords, in his 1998 speech attacking Labour's plans to do away with hereditary peers. He argued that the public would be better represented by 'amateurs' rather than 'professional politicians.' Predictably, this set off a debate that if choice by lot and amateur politicians are so beneficial, why not go the whole hog and replace the lottery of birth with a genuine lottery? Supporters argued that its very randomness would itself ensure peers were much more representative in terms of age, gender, geographical spread, ethnic, social and political background. A weekly lottery draw with the prize of a seat in the House of Lords was even suggested – with the safeguard that no-one be permitted to buy more than one ticket per week. This would prevent a wealthy individual, in an innovative take on the cash-for-peerages scandal, from beating the odds by spending millions of pounds on lottery tickets. A modest start has been made in local elections, where councils are allowed to reward voters with tickets for draws offering prizes such as free membership of local authority gyms or sports clubs.

A more strategic approach came from the think-tank Demos, in its 1998 pamphlet *The Athenian Option*. Drawing on the ancient Greek experience, it recommended randomly appointing ordinary citizens for the House of Lords through a national lottery. Under this system, designed to create a truly representative second chamber free from party politics, those selected would serve for a fixed term as 'Peers in Parliament'. In order to ensure equal numbers of men and women and fair representation from all regions, selection from among registered voters would be weighted appropriately. So, in that sense, it is not entirely random. The process would take place by stages until ultimately a majority of peers are chosen by lot. Support, too, is growing for selecting members of quangos and other public bodies randomly in order to open them up to scrutiny.

Selection by lot has also been suggested for local council seats to counter-balance state centralisation by both Tories and Labour, for a second chamber of the European Parliament, and even for elections in Iraq, though the last is almost certainly a bridge too far. Possibly because of the deep ambivalence of governments who fear irrationality and loss of control, the role of random selection as an agent of change, helping the societies which use it, has long been neglected. I hope this little book has helped to redress the balance. For it is a racing certainty that for centuries to come, financial, political and social lotteries – and in forms we can only now guess at – will continue to determine fates.

AND TODAY'S QUESTION IS "ARE
'PHONE-INS' (A) A LOTTERY (B) A CON
(C) A STITCH-UP OR (D) ALL THREE?"

Rollover 1

SCAMS ANCIENT AND MODERN

Ancient

'So many Sharpers, Swindlers and Cheats find encouragement in this great metropolis', complained the London magistrate, Patrick Colquhoun, in a 1796 diatribe against the game. Some of the more notorious fiddles were …

Dividing tickets to a ridiculous degree

In eighteenth-century Britain stockbrokers marketed state lottery tickets by dividing them into shares. As each ticket seldom cost below £10 (a huge sum then), this meant everyone could take part. The novelist Daniel Defoe, who was a trustee for a 1695 lottery, went further and urged the radical step that tickets be sold directly to the public 'to pay off a Hundred Thousand Pounds of Debt'.

Unfortunately, division was carried to such extremes, to sixty-fourths even, that the system was abused. The law was amended in 1788 to impose a fine £50 (£2,500 today) on anyone who divided a ticket other than by a half, quarter, eighth or sixteenth. The odds of winning a prize of £10 were 1 in 20,000.

Betting on Lottery Numbers

An invidious, widespread and illegal form of betting spread after 1775 which involved a complicated system known as 'insuring', whereby bets were placed on the likelihood of a stated number being drawn on a certain day. The lure was that in return for, say, a shilling, a pound would be paid on a specified number. The relatively low stakes meant working class people could afford to play, but the schemes were mainly fraudulent. Insuring was a major reason why the state lottery was abolished in 1826.

Betting on the numbers which may come up in the National Lottery is still strictly prohibited in Britain today (though bookmakers allow punters to bet on the outcome of overseas lotteries).

Bribery

Tickets were usually drawn from large wooden 'wheels' (strong boxes) by the Bluecoat boys of Christ's Hospital over a long period of time, the technology then being lacking to ensure a faster and more protected process. Their performance did not please everyone; after a visit to the 1710 draw the satirist Jonathan Swift described them as self-satisfied 'jackanapes'. Attempts to corrupt and bribe the boys were rife. In 1775 a man was charged with attempting to suborn two boys during the draw of a lottery to dispose of jeweller James Cox's collection of automata. In the same year another boy was convicted of concealing ticket number 21,481 in his sleeve, to be produced later as a prize. Elaborate precautions were then implemented. A Treasury regulation insisted before each ticket was drawn the boy be inspected to see 'that his pockets be sewed up and … he shall keep his left hand in his girdle behind him and his right hand open with his fingers extended.'

Cheats corrupted others, such as the bell-ringer at St Clement's Church in London who was bribed to put the church clock back by five minutes. His associates, having learned the winning numbers of the day at the Guildhall draw, would then hurry to the lottery houses and put money on those numbers before the clock signalled the deadline for placing bets.

Extortionists took advantage of the fact that any member of the public had the power, and could thereby earn £500, by shopping a neighbour for taking illegal bets on lottery numbers. This caused 'hundreds of persons to be sworn into prison, upon the oaths or pretended oaths of people that could not afterwards be found', according to one report.

Forgery

Tickets were often forged. In 1777, two Jewish landlords Samuel Noah and Joseph Aarones appeared before the lord mayor of London accused of changing a ticket numbered 23,590 to 25,590, which won a £2,000 prize. Although the forgery, brilliantly executed, was itself undetected, the crime was discovered by a chance meeting; the fraudsters, however, were acquitted as their accomplices supported, on oath, their claim to have found the ticket. But at the same sessions, Daniel Denny was found guilty of the capital offence of altering a lottery ticket with intent to defraud.

Forgery was also a serious offence in the United States, where crooks sometimes turned this to their advantage. A player in Germantown, Pennsylvania, was delighted to win a major prize in the early 1800s until three men frightened him into thinking his ticket was forged and he gave it up. They claimed the prize, but were later discovered and convicted. Today, the barcode on lottery tickets makes forgery practically impossible as it is swiftly detected.

Fake tickets

Thousands of people, particularly in country towns and villages, were regularly duped by a simple ruse. They would pay out, usually in public houses, small sums of money to travelling salesmen of lottery tickets and be given, in return, receipts stating the buyer was a subscriber to the actual purchase of a ticket or stamped share of it. These were worthless pieces of paper with no legal validity if the ticket won a prize. Money was paid only to the ticket holder.

Fake Lottery Societies

Societies were set up which enabled players to club together to purchase tickets, just as people do today in their workplace or social club. The most well-known were The Amicable Society of Lottery Adventurers, the United Lottery Society and the Union and Laudable Society of Lottery Adventurers.

Others were a front. They would copy the terms of real societies to fool the unwary, forge their certificates, and sell a few tickets with the same numbers indefinitely, if buyers could be found. In 1784, fraudsmen even took over the defunct offices of the Amicable Society at No. 4 Exchange Alley, a narrow street between Lombard Street and Cornhill, and pretended to be its representatives. On this occasion, they were detected. Outside London particularly, they often were not.

Fake Lotteries

Sometimes the entire lottery was a fiction. In 1723, a lottery proposed for Harburgh (a town in Hanover) was said to help maintain two-way trade between England and George I's German dominions. It was claimed, falsely, that the King endorsed and supported it. Many investors were deceived and lost huge amounts of money to this fraud which a Christian apologist and corrupt politician, John Shute, first Viscount Barrington in the Irish peerage and MP for Berwick, had promoted. He was unmasked and expelled from the Commons.

Impossible conditions

Players were sometimes offered tickets for an extraordinarily low price. But impossible conditions were always attached, such as the ticket only being valid for a few hours during a forty-two-day drawing or to win the £20,000 the number had to be the first drawn on a particular day. 'Events not likely ever to happen in twenty thousand years', as the Amicable Society's lottery guide of 1786 put it. Such conditions were hardly ever made clear.

Sales Tricks

Dishonest salesmen sold ticket numbers which they knew would turn out to be blank, or tickets that were not theirs to sell.(If the latter did win a major prize, the salesman disappeared smartly). Sometimes the same ticket was sold to two people. In a 1767 case, the player who found that he didn't hold the real ticket after all went mad.

Another trick was to advertise additional personal prizes paid out of the pocket of the lottery operators themselves, such as 'eight pipes of the best port wine'. When winners came to collect they were told that, unfortunately, the organizers had since discovered that such bonuses were forbidden by law.

Sometimes a broker would refuse to honour prizes. In *The Flying Post* of 26 July 1698, an advertisement warned subscribers to a lottery called 'The Wheel of Fortune' to get their money back if they bought tickets from Robert Wolfe, a distiller in Leadenhall Market. It said simply 'he will not pay', for reasons undisclosed.

Other charlatans would claim to foresee winning tickets. *The Universal Spectator* of 23 November 1731 recounts the story of a cunning woman who had lived in a garret and made a living telling fortunes through divining coffee gourds in a cup. She had now moved to the first floor and kept a footman, selling advice to lottery players on the most lucky tickets to buy. She promised a maid called Kate that a £10 ticket, which she spent her savings acquiring, was certain to win a £1,000 prize. This prompted Kate to tell her long-standing employer 'to get another Servant as she intended to be Nobody's Slave much longer'. The ticket, of course, won nothing.

Other self-proclaimed seers were not so grasping. The Mystic Meg of the 1710 draw, an astrologer called Dr Langham operating in Moorfields, East London, charged half a crown for a prediction, but sportingly allowed eighteen pence to be paid from any prize won.

Inflating Profits

There was often a huge difference between the 'contract price' of tickets (the price lottery contractors paid the treasury for them) and the price at which contractors resold them to retailers. As virtually no controls existed on resales, contractors had total market control and were able to rip off the public.

On occasion, they conspired to make sham sales of lottery tickets to each other at a price higher or lower than the market in order to raise or deflate the current price. 'A.B.' (1811's 'Disgusted of Tunbridge Wells') exposed this practice in a series of letters to *The Times*, pointing out that the contractors 'go out from Downing-street, armed as it were, with a special commission empowering them to take advantage of everybody.'

Misleading Adverts

Adverts for lottery schemes were deliberately misleading. They often implied there was a four to one chance of winning a prize (the real odds were always much greater) and, by sleight of hand mathematics, implied that the number of prizes available was much higher than was the case. Large bonuses, to be shared among all ticket-holders, were sometimes promised but never paid. One player, happily hurrying to the lottery office to pick up his bonus in 1816, found it was worth just five pence and a farthing.

It was no good complaining if you felt cheated. There was simply no customer complaints procedure. In 1811, one man was defrauded of a £20,000 prize and attempted to protest, but he could not even discover the names of the twenty-six state-appointed lottery commissioners employed to ensure fair play.

'Get rich quick' books

Then as now, enterprising businessmen sold advice on how to win. Their pamphlets did a brisk trade among gullible players who rarely seemed to wonder why the writer did not keep the secret to himself. One publication, circulating in 1795 and claiming to compress 600 pages of mathematical mumbo jumbo into

30, was snappily entitled *Calculations and Facts relative to Lottery Insurances and Demonstrative of the Striking Advantages of pursuing particular plans*.

It argued that the primitive lottery wheels distorted the draw as the 40,000 tickets, extracted at the rate of 1,000 a day for forty days 'press each other into mass, reciprocally binding each other with edges'. That made it impossible for them, initially, to be mixed up properly as the numbers, traditionally cut into batches of a 1,000, stayed in the order they were first placed until there was more space in the wheels. From this simple observation the author constructed a betting plan based on the premise that the best time to buy tickets was between a third and two-thirds the way through the draw.

He was certainly correct about the cumbersome wheels. When the lottery draw was completed at the Guildhall on Thursday 5 January 1744, ticket number 11,053 was drawn last and, as was the custom, declared entitled to a £1,000 prize. The owner's joy was short-lived. For when the wheels were taken back to store in Whitehall and opened up, ticket number 72,248 was found stuck in a crevice, and thus declared last out. On other occasions when tickets were suspected to be missing a Bluecoat boy was often stripped naked and squeezed into the wheel to find them, in an interesting variant on the abuse of young chimney sweeps.

Clandestine Houses

Although there was an inspector of lottery houses, his work was cut out to regulate the many illegal premises around London. They made huge profits from lottery wheels which were often rigged; their insides concealed ingenious springs and strips of gum which threw out or retained tickets to order.

These so-called 'offices' were often marked by a large number upon the windows or upon a green curtain or blind protected by an oak plank and plated with iron. A man with an alarm bell would alert the arrival of the inspectors, allowing staff to flee through the back door or over the roofs. Sometimes, the thugs who guarded the door fought back. On Sunday 24 February 1788 a lengthy pitched battle took place at a house in Whitechapel between Justice Hyde and his party of men and doorkeepers armed with staves, cutlasses, pistols and blunderbusses all 'offering stout resistance'.

Disorder was endemic even outside the regulated premises; hundreds of people regularly jostled for admission during the forty-day draw. And, in the coffee shops, pickpockets dipped for rich rewards. 'Monday night, an eminent Stock-broker had his pocket picked in Jonathan's Coffee House of fifty lottery tickets, the value of which, at the present price, is above £700', said a news report for Wednesday 18 November 1767.

Some unlicensed firms made such huge profits that they felt confident enough to operate openly, even advertising their illegal game in the press .One such was 'Shergold & Co', run by a woman, which thrived in the 1790s despite repeated public exposures.

Corrupt Lottery Inspectors

Many of the dozens of officials paid to ensure draws were conducted properly and honestly were corrupt, including their leader Thomas Wood, Inspector of Lotteries since 1789. An 1808 Parliamentary enquiry suspected that he dishonestly organised the Government's annual contracts with lottery operators and turned a blind eye to his staff receiving bribes from the unlicensed lottery house keepers. 'I am confident that he winks and connives at illegal insurances', one prominent broker told the MPs.

Wood, who was seen 'daily and nightly' in the company of the gangs, was certainly ineffective. Once, in a fit of pique and at great public expense, he arrested 400 people for insuring lottery tickets, but most turned out to be innocent charladies and washerwomen who had to be released. Wood was put on indefinite 'gardening leave', suffered a nervous breakdown in 1812 and the following year, in full view of the public, assaulted acting inspector Obadiah Hesse at a lottery draw.

Morocco Men

The spivs who promoted illegal 'insuring' in public houses and coffee shops, receiving up to ten per cent in commission, were known as 'Morocco Men' because they carried flashy leather red wallets.

According to Colquhoun, in 1800 there were nearly 7,500 of them. Generally regarded as 'a mixture of the gentleman and debauchee', they were often smooth-talking high class conmen down on their luck; their nearest social equivalent of more recent times were the Remittance Men, dubious minor aristocrats and gentlemen banished by their families to the further reaches of the British Empire on a retainer.

They operated everywhere from city slum to the most picturesque village, often using milkmen to solicit bets from servants when they delivered the milk. The Victorian chronicler, John Francis, reported they could be seen:

> In the old hall of the country gentleman, in the mansion of the city merchant, in the buttery of the rural squire, in the homestead of the farmer, among the reapers as they worked on the hillside … They whispered temptation to the innocent; they hinted at fraud to the novice. They lured the youthful; they excited the aged; and no place was so pure and no spot so degraded, but, for love of 7 and a half per cent, did the Morocco man mark it with his pestilential presence.

When imprisoned, which was often, they lived well and usually dined with their warders because their employers, the illegal lottery operators, always ensured they received two guineas a week during their sentence.

Evangelical tracts published lurid warnings of the fate of their victims. One told of a young girl who became a lottery addict:

> To drown her Reflections, and stupefy her Senses, she drinks Drams; which, with the diseases she accumulates from frequent Prostitution, soon puts an end to her miserable life.

Punishments

Between 1783 and 1802 more than 1,000 people were imprisoned in Britain for offences against the lottery acts, but many more were not convicted when they came to court since witnesses were generally intimidated. Punishment for forging and counterfeiting tickets was extreme, with offenders hanged or transported. Many were put in the pillory to be pelted by the mob.

Not a fraud (1776)

Lottery laws were often badly drafted, their ambiguity regularly making it impossible to know what was permitted. In 1776, a bookseller called Johnson launched *The Lottery Magazine*, an attractively produced compendium of literary, political and commercial intelligence selling for one shilling and modestly billed as 'the most extraordinary work that ever appeared in any age or nation'. The gimmick was that each issue included three or four vouchers that related to the current national draw.

A lottery office keeper called Price (not Charles 'Patch' Price) who feared competition informed against him. In a case heard at Bow Street Magistrates Court in 1777 his counsel, Fielding, claimed that Johnson had broken an obscure law passed under George I. Johnson's counsel, Morgan, argued that the magazine was not promoting a lottery but simply, as a marketing ploy, supplying several numbered vouchers per issue for a specific 100 guineas to be given, in the case of those numbers coming up, as prizes of £10,000 and £20,000. The magistrate threw the case out.

An Ancient Chinese Custom

Perhaps the most entertaining overseas fraud was the Wai Seng lottery of Canton province. This raised money for the provincial treasury, and was hugely popular in nineteenth-century China.

You bet by guessing the largest number of surnames of the successful competitors in the fiendishly difficult annual examinations for the Chinese civil service. Wai Seng guides, the equivalent of horse racing tips today, were produced as to the form of the candidates, but the odds were sometimes rigged through a process called Kam Seng (suppressing surnames). Betting syndicates would bribe the would-be mandarins to drop out of the exams, which they could always take the following year. In 1890, the lottery office itself was caught nobbling candidates and heavily fined.

Postscript
In 2007, two bank managers in China were arrested after stealing £3 million and spending most of it on the state lottery in a vain attempt to win the jackpot.

Modern

Scams today are just as inventive as they were in the eighteenth century. Or indeed 2,000 years earlier, when corrupt Roman magistrates weighted small wooden 'lots' drawn from urns.

Robbed by Post
Phoney lottery and prize draw mailshots arriving in the post from overseas are an increasing menace. The victims are mainly the UK's elderly citizens who collectively lose up to £100 million a year. The scams are designed to look like offers from legitimate organisations but addresses quoted turn out to be maildrops, most of the companies do not exist and the signatures on letters are false. Cash, typically £20 or £50, is demanded to make a claim and often sending it proves just the prelude to far greater claims. Once a confused elderly person replies with cash, he or she is bombarded with other fraudulent letters, sometimes as many as 100 a week.

The postal rip-offs have grown so much that the Government routinely warns consumers to throw the scams into the recycling bin. One imaginative campaign involved sending out 20,000 fake prize draw mailings promising recipients in the Midlands, South East, North East and Wales that they had won a guaranteed £15,000.

The letters, under the false name of 'SuperMegaLotto', were personalised to make it appear exclusive to each household, which was urged to act quickly to claim its prize. When opened they contained detailed official advice designed to drive home the message that such mailings are frauds. The European Commission has also launched a clampdown on con artists using cross-border scams such as bogus holiday clubs and phoney lottery and sweepstakes.

Yet people continue to be taken in. Every year British consumers lose £260 million to fake foreign lotteries, according to the Office for Fair Trading. There have been tragedies. In 2003, a technician at Anglia Polytechnic University doused himself with petrol and set fire to himself in a field near Cambridge on his forty-eighth birthday after learning that he was the victim of a lottery scam. He thought he could repay his huge debts after receiving an email from an Amsterdam-based internet lottery saying he had won £658,000, but had first to set up a new bank account. As has happened to so many others so cruelly deceived, he then found he could not access the money allegedly deposited.

Fiddling the draw

Because of modern technology such as computerised betting systems and sophisticated safeguards, scandals are very rare today in state-regulated lotteries in North America and Europe. In 1982, crooks, including the TV host, attempted to defraud the Pennsylvania lottery by injecting with fluid some of the balls used to determine the winning numbers at the draw. This dodge made them heavier and thus more likely to drop out first from the selection machine. They were quickly found out.

In the UK, a shopkeeper once used the cancellation mechanism on his terminal to void tickets after which he smartly pocketed the bets. Today, it is very difficult to tamper with the mechanics of the UK lottery. The latex rubber balls shown shooting out the numbers at the climax of the televised draw are regularly examined by the Office of National Weights and Measures Laboratory and the machines are tested annually to ensure they work properly.

It is a different matter with private, unregulated lotteries. More than 300 extremely profitable private lotteries were spawned in Russia following the collapse of the Soviet Union. The overwhelming majority were totally unregulated, many were run by the Russian mafia, fraud and corruption flourished. Yet one in two Russians played these crooked games, which a Moscow police officer, Sgt Pavel Dyanbenko described as 'One of the biggest rip-offs that exists on earth.'

TV quiz prize shows

Allegedly 'interactive' TV quiz shows, usually starting at pub closing time, are often disguised lotteries as the questions are so easy virtually no skill is required to answer them.

The system works through the broadcasters, mainly ITV and small cable and satellite production companies, using minor celebrities to egg on callers to pay 70p a try on their phone bill, but with no guarantee of actually getting on the show. Instead, a computer randomly selects the callers who might total as many as 6,000 every sixty seconds, with the odds of being connected to a studio about 400 to 1. Minutes go by before the 'correct answer' to such simple questions as 'What is the capital of Britain?' is finally broadcast – misleading thousands of viewers into thinking they alone know the answer. So they redial in the hope of a prize which can range from £20 to £100,000, running up large phone bills which are hugely profitable for the companies. The quiz channels, including the digital channel ITV Play and ITV's early hours show *The Mint* (both scrapped in 2007) have made huge profits.

The all-party Commons Culture, Media and Sport Committee, which investigated the quizzes in 2007, was shocked by what it found and called for stronger regulation. Shortly after, mainstream daytime television was also exposed for cheating viewers out of tens of thousands of pounds. The popular *You Say, We Pay* competition on Channel 4's *Richard and Judy Show* was pulled after the *Mail on Sunday* newspaper claimed viewers were being urged to enter the £1-a-time game even though contestants had already been chosen. However, the show's husband and wife hosts, Richard Madeley and Judy Finnegan, were not aware of the way an average of 15,000 people a day were conned into believing they had a chance of competing for a cash prize. In a dramatic move, ITV pulled the plug on its quiz channel ITV Play and suspended all premium-rate interactive services pending the outcome of an independent review. All premium rate phone calls, text votes and red button interaction in such popular series as *X Factor, I'm a Celebrity Get Me Out of Here* and *Dancing on Ice* were cancelled. The shows eventually returned, save ITV Play which had brought in £54 million revenue in 2006.

Yet the list of abuses continued to lengthen, severely damaging trust between broadcaster and audience; Channel Five admitted winners' names on its show *Brainteaser* were sometimes made up and a major scandal blew up over Britain's most popular break-fast television show, *GMTV*. It ended the contract with Opera Interactive Technology, the company running its competitions, when it was found to be finalizing short lists of entrants before the deadline for callers expired. The practice of picking winners early was alleged to have swindled viewers out of £10 million a year over a four-year period.

The watchdogs bit back. The official media regulator Ofcom fined the BBC £50,000 for faking a phone quiz winner on its trusted children's show *Blue Peter*. Later, the BBC suspended all its phone-in competitions after uncovering a 'hornet's nest of decep-tion' involving flagship programmes such as the Comic Relief and Children in Need appeals. New rules were imposed to make quiz shows tell callers how much they are spending and the real odds of getting through to the studio.

The Gambling Commission also declared the shows were really lotteries and therefore liable to pay more tax, with twenty per cent of profits going to good causes. Hopes that the TV quiz industry, worth an estimated £160 million a year, will regulate itself seem, however, remote as companies are unlikely to give up easy alternative revenues at a time when TV advertising is declining. The 2005 Gaming Act, which came into force in September 2007, is unlikely to squash this blatant exploitation of consumers; it was drafted before the shows became a broadcasting fact of life. Telling viewers the precise chances of their call getting through is a key first step. So is Ofcom's determination to fine heavily the offending broadcasters; nearly £10 million, as of July 2008. But only when the issue is taken to court, and case law established, will this abuse be properly squashed.

Footnote

In their defence, the shows could well claim viewers are not that bright. On a BBC regional radio quiz in 2006, a contestant was asked which famous former foreign leader (Bill Clinton) addressed the recent Labour Party Conference. The contestant replied 'Lenin'.

Skimming off charity cash

Given the huge amount of money handed out to good causes from the UK National Lottery, fraudsters will inevitably continue to submit bogus applications for grants to the distributing bodies. The gangs use false names and addresses, and generally claim to represent small community groups based in urban areas, cleverly not asking for too much so as not to arouse suspicion.

In 2004, the bank accounts of thirty registered charities were frozen as Scotland Yard investigated allegedly fraudulent lottery payments of more than £1 million across the charitable and voluntary sector. Other well-known funding bodies, such as BBC Children in Need, Barnado's and Comic Relief were also believed to have been targeted. Since then, following a National Audit Office report, stricter security checks on grant applications have been introduced.

The Big Lottery Fund, which spotted the original irregularities when it took over the New Opportunities Fund and the Community Fund, is confident its sophisticated firewalls will detect any criminal activity. But the more than £600 million it distributes each year – half the money for good causes – will always be a challenge for crooked claimants.

Not a fraud (2005)

All is sometimes not what it seems in the crazy lottery world. In 2005 in the United States the Powerball Multi-State Lottery quickly suspected fraud when 110 players from twenty-nine states all became second prize winners in exactly the same way. Each of them was entitled to US $500,000 dollars for getting the same five out of six numbers right: 22, 28, 32, 33 and 39. Statistically there should only have been four or five. Desperately, the Lottery owners searched everywhere for an explanation. But none of the newspaper forecast columns had printed the numbers, and there was no clue elsewhere.

It was only when the winners started arriving at their office to claim their prizes that the mystery was finally solved. They had all eaten in Chinese restaurants all over America and had all chosen their lucky numbers from a fortune cookie. All the cookies came from the same factory, Wonton Food in Long Island City. Derek Wong of Wonton Foods later said:

> We make four million fortune cookies each day, and sell them to restaurants all over the country, but we don't change the numbers very often. It's nice that 110 ten people won the lottery because of our cookies, but from now on we've been told to use a computer to make sure that the numbers are random because it will be more efficient.

Rollover 2

FROM FIELDING TO DALZIEL AND PASCOE

From Henry Fielding's 1732 satire *The Lottery* to British television's BBC1 detective drama *Dalziel and Pascoe* (where racetrack murders hinged on a big lottery win in a 2006 episode) the luck of the draw has inspired plays, songs, films, TV, novels, poems, and paintings.

As early as 1660 Edward Ford's satirical ballad, *Fair Play in the Lottery*, drew the crowds at Drury Lane, who cheered jokes about the trumpet blasts preceding each announcement of a winner: *Trumpet* … 'Give me a lot old boy, and there's a shilling'.

Fielding's farce was very popular, especially when the lottery was being drawn at the Guildhall. In Scene One, Mr Stocks sings:

> Lottery is a Taxation,
> Upon all the Fools in Creation;
> And Heav'n be prais'd,
> It is easily rais'd,
> Credulity's always in Fashion:
> For, Folly's a Fund,
> Will never lose Ground,
> While Fools are so rife in the nation.

Fielding, whose half-brother the blind magistrate Sir John Fielding supplied him with first hand experience of the effects of lottery losses on the poor, also mentions the game in his novel *Tom Jones*. So does Daniel Defoe in *Moll Flanders*, Jane Austen in *Pride and Prejudice*, Emily Brontë in *Wuthering Heights,* and William Makepeace Thackeray in *Vanity Fair*.

The Gentleman's Magazine of 4 May 1734 published a spoof Bill which proposed 'all the Virgins in Great Britain from the age of 15 to 40 shall be disposed of by lottery.' Tickets were to be available to all men earning more than £100 per year and 'no women of scandalous or lewd behaviour shall be put in it.' Several readers thought this a splendid idea and wrote in to support it. Fourteen years earlier, another satirical lottery, *A Good Husband for Five Shillings*, was published by Isaac Bickerstaff (the pseudonym used by Sir Richard Steele, founder of *The Spectator* and later by the satirist Jonathan Swift). This proposed to remedy the scarcity of husbands caused by the French wars by offering 1,000 tickets at five shillings each to all 'single ladies, Widows or Maids.' The top prize was a 'Modern Whig' worth £2,000 a year and 'very strong in the loins'.

The lottery was, literally, in the limelight during the late eighteenth century and early nineteenth century with numerous productions. At the Haymarket Theatre in 1791 a comedy called *The School for Arrogance* began with a prologue spoken by a news vendor satirically announcing the lottery:

Here are promotions, dividends, rewards,
A list of bankrupts, and of new made lords

In 1802, a farce in two acts, *Lottery Prize*, was performed in both London and Dublin. News that his ticket numbered 2,538 has won a £10,000 prize in the English lottery turns the head of an Irish apothecary, Lenitive. He behaves obnoxiously to his servant, patients, acquaintances and fiancée until he discovers number 2,538 was a blank after all, by which time of course his life has been ruined. Audiences would have found this twist entirely plausible; errors were often made. Charles Lamb tells the true story of a gentleman walking along Cheapside when he sees ticket number 1,069 advertised in large figures on a lottery house window as winning the first prize of £20,000. It is his ticket. The lucky winner spends ten minutes walking round St Paul's to compose himself and returns, only to find the winning number altered to 10,069. A clerk had confused the digit.

In 1826, the year of England's 'last lottery', a vaudeville entitled *La Maison en Loterie* by Picard and Rodet drew crowds to the French Theatre in London. Perlet played the central character, an Iago-like lawyer's clerk called Malin Bossu. According to one review, he exhibited

> an elfin-like, unearthly malice, in the evil tricks which he seems
> – from pure whim – to be always putting upon everybody; and
> the scenes in which he opens the letter containing the account of
> the fate of his lottery ticket, displayed serious powers … of a very
> considerable order.

Two centuries later another morality tale was told in the form of the British television comedy drama *At Home with the Braithwaites*, which became an instant hit. Alison Braithwaite, a suburban house-wife from Leeds, wins the £38 million EuroLottery prize but tries to keep her good fortune secret from her greedy, dysfunctional family because she fears it will corrupt them. Of course the truth eventually emerges – and the family falls apart. Moral: a big lottery win does not buy happiness, but it does make an award-winning TV show with record ratings over four series. It might also have given the idea of keeping quiet about a lottery bonanza to the mystery woman who took part, under the pseudonym 'Jane' in a BBC Radio Five Live phone-in on money and happiness. The mother of two revealed she had still not told her husband of her £1.5 million win three years previously because he would have wanted to give up work and thus 'destroy the little family unit we've got now'. Only one in four win-ners ever agrees to go public in the UK National Lottery.

In *Lost*, a baffling US drama television series that follows the survivors of a plane crash onto a mysterious tropical island, the lottery numbers 4, 8, 15, 16, 23 and 42 have a star role. They appear throughout both in sequence and individually and their sum, 108, becomes significant.

Dozens of other television series use the draw as a dramatic device. In a 2002 episode of British television's popular police series *The Bill*, PC Reg Hollis makes a huge blunder when he changes a winning number in the weekly entry of Sun Hill police station. In a 2007 episode of BBC TV's hospital drama *Holby City* Nurse Donna wins a £20,000 lottery prize and hands in her notice saying her life will not be affected.

Stage plays include John Godber's *Lucky Sods,* which tells the story of married couple Morris and Joan who never take the lottery seriously until they win a £2 million prize. Although the windfall initially brings them great joy, they soon realize their lives have been changed for the worst.

Lotteries play a major role in fiction. In the surreal 1904 novel *The Napoleon of Notting Hill* by the English writer G.K. Chesterton, the King is chosen by lot. Even more surreal is the 1941 fable *The Lottery in Babylon* by the Argentine writer Jorge Luis Borges, which describes a fictional society where everyone's destiny changes every sixty days by means of a lottery (taken to be a metaphor for God or the role of chance in life). The American novelist and short story writer, Shirley Jackson, became famous for her chilling story *The Lottery*, which was made into a radio, television and one-act stage play, ballet, short film and opera. This dark tale of the evil just lurking beneath the surface of everyday life caused a flood of protests when it was first published in the *New Yorker* in 1948. Many readers cancelled their subscriptions and others sent the author hate mail after reading of events in a typical small American town where a sacrificial victim is chosen each year in a public lottery and then stoned to death.

Graham Greene's satire on capitalism, *Doctor Fischer of Geneva, or The Bomb Plot,* is equally dark and was also made into a TV film. Like the mad Roman emperors, the wealthy Dr Fischer humiliates his sycophantic dinner party guests by offering them Christmas crackers which have either large cheques or a bomb in them.

The plot of the lighter 1997 comic thriller *Lucky You* by Carl Hiaasen, American writer of Florida fantasies, depends entirely on a lottery win awarded to JoLayne Lucks, a poor African-American woman. In Luke Rhinehart's subversive 1972 novel *The Dice Man,* a bored renegade psychiatrist makes all his decisions, large and small, by rolling dice. The book, which has become a cult classic, makes the point that when a life is ruled entirely by chance, anything can happen. Twenty years later he wrote a sequel, *The Search for the Dice Man,* followed in 2000 by *The Book of the Die,* a playful handbook for his risk-taking followers said to number hundreds of thousands. In 2008, Patricia Wood's novel *Lottery,* about a special needs' lottery winner dealing with claims on his wealth, was short-listed for the 13th Orange Prize.

Science fiction writers have followed suit. In his 1986 novel, *The Songs of Distant Earth,* Arthur C. Clarke sets the action on a far-flung planet Thalassia, colonised by human beings whose embryos had been launched into space to avoid the imminent death of the sun. They establish a utopian society where the main instrument in achieving fairness and justice for all is a computerised random selection programme to appoint leaders. Not everyone approves, and particularly not the unambitious manufacturer of sporting equipment who found himself compulsorily selected as President of Thalassia.

Philip K Dick's quirky novel, *Solar Lottery,* set in the year 2203, also turns on a sophisticated lottery which picks both public office-holders and the targets of political assassinations, central attraction of a reality TV show watched worldwide. All goes well until it throws up Ted Benteley, a maverick who challenges the system. He had one chance out of six billion of being selected, which looks impossible. Yet, in real life, such odds have been beaten. In 2006 Valerie Gibson, a mother of three from Long Island in the United States, won the $1 million jackpot in the New York lottery jubilee game. Four years previously she bought the winning ticket in the state's 'Cool Million' scratchcard game. To hit the $1 million jackpot twice, she had to overcome odds of 1 in 3.7 billion.

The lottery has always inspired painters (even Picasso indirectly; he won a goat in a lottery in 1950 and thereafter made goats a major theme in his work). In 1600, the Dutch oil painter, David Vinckboons portrayed with Bruegel-like detail, the raffling of objects at a country fair. Another Dutch artist, Gillis Coignet, executed a beautiful oil painting of spectators watching a lottery being drawn at night in Amsterdam, *Drawing of the 1592 Lottery on "The Russland", in Aid of the Lunatic Asylum.* Twenty-five years later his compatriot, Claes Jansz. Visscher, made a print, circulated in Haarlem and Amsterdam, promoting a lottery for a new almshouse in Egmond-op-Zee, hard hit by war and floods. The delicate engraving depicts, without irony, a poor fisherman and his wife holding up a board displaying luxury goods and prizes such as precious goblets and tapestries. Vincent van Gogh's 1890 watercolour, *Waiting for the results of the draw at the lottery office,* shows a back view of a group of working-class people hovering anxiously by the door as they await their fate. Many other engravings and lithographs illustrate the game's social impact, some jolly but mostly grim such as an early nineteenth-century lithograph by the German artist Motte depicting a hanged man. It is captioned, *The only solution for the loser.*

Lottery engravings by William Hogarth are surprisingly pedestrian compared to his more familiar satirical works *Gin Lane* and *The Harlot's Progress.* Perhaps he had a soft spot for the draw; he used one to dispose of his famous painting of the 1745 Rebellion, *The March to Finchley* (1749), claiming this was 'the only way a living painter has any probability of being tolerably paid for his time'. He sold 1,843 tickets and gave the remaining 157 to London's Foundling Hospital, where he was a hardworking governor. Rather suspiciously, at the draw on Monday 30 April 1750, ticket number 1,941 belonging to the hospital came up and the governors were given this remarkable painting that night.

Twentieth-century cartoons are invariably entertaining and light-hearted. Before the return of the national lottery to Britain, they featured the Irish Sweepstake, National Savings Premium Bonds, football pools and bingo. Thereafter targets included the first lottery regulator politicians, Camelot's 'fat cat' directors awarding themselves huge bonuses, and often controversial awards of lottery money. Forgotten or lost tickets, unclaimed winnings, and large prizes ruining lives continue to be popular themes. But in the early days the favourite jokes were based on Camelot's first gimmick, the pointing finger attached to a disembodied hand under the slogan 'It Could Be You', centrepiece of the iconic advertising campaign.

BIBLIOGRAPHY
AND SOURCES

General

Ackroyd, Peter, *London, The Biography*, London, 2000
Ashton, John, *A History of English Lotteries*, London, 1893
Athenian Mercury
Bruno, Bernard, *Lotteries in Europe*, Brussels, 1994
Dickson, Peter, *The financial revolution in England 1688–1756*, London, 1967
Douglas, Andrew, *British Charitable Gambling 1956–1994*, London, 1995
EL, European State Lotteries and Toto Associations, www.european-lotteries.org
Ewen, Cecil L'Estrange, *Lotteries and Sweepstakes*, London, 1932
Flying Post
Grant Geoffrey, *English State Lotteries 1694–1826*, London, 2001
La Fleur's World Lottery Almanac, 2007
NASPL, North American Association of State and Provincial Lotteries, www.naspl.org
Oxford Dictionary of National Biography
Smith, Colin & Monkcom, Stephen, *The Law of Betting, Gaming and Lotteries*, London, 1987
The Annual Register
The Gentleman's Magazine
The London Gazette
The London Evening Post
The Times
WL, World Lottery Association, www.world.lotteries.org

1. Greek Gods

Amandry, Pierre, *La Mantique apollinienne:essai sur le fonctionnement de l'oracle à Delphes*, Paris, 1950
Aristotle's Politics, trans. Richard Robinson, Harmondsworth, 1962
Athenian Constitution, The, trans. Peter Rhodes, Harmondsworth, 1984
Connelly, Joan, *Portrait of a Priestess*, Princeton USA, 2007
Headlam, James, *Election by Lot at Athens*, Cambridge, 1933
Homer, *The Iliad*, book VII, 207–228, trans. Alexander Pope, Harmondsworth, 1996

Parke, Herbert & Wormell, Donald, *The Delphic Oracle*, Oxford, 1956
Robbins, Frank, 'The Lot Oracle at Delphi', *Classical Philology*, vol. XI (1916), pp 278–292
Staveley, Eastland, *Greek and Roman Voting and Elections*, London, 1972

2. Roman Emperors

Dio, Cassius, *Roman History*, trans. Earnest Cary, Loeb Classical Library, 1961
Everitt, Anthony, *The First Emperor: Caesar Augustus and the Triumph of Rome*, London, 2006
Grant, Michael, *The Roman Emperors*, London, 1997
Hay, John, *The Amazing Emperor Heliogabalus*, London, 1911
Scriptores Historiae Augustae, trans. David Magie, London, 1967
Strong, Roy, *Feast: A History of Grand Eating*, London, 2002
Suetonius, *The Twelve Caesars*, trans. Robert Graves, London, 1957
Tacitus, *The Annals of Ancient Rome*, trans. Michael Grant, London, 1959

3. Mathematicians from Mesopotamia

Bernstein, Peter, *Against the Gods; the remarkable story of risk*, New York, 1996
Kaplan, Robert, *The Nothing That Is. A Natural History of the Zero*, London, 1999
Seife, Charles, *Zero: the biography of a dangerous idea*, London, 2003

4. It Could Be Ye

Bray, William, 'Account of the Lottery of 1567', *Archaeologia* XIX (1821), pp 79–87
Dietz, Frederick, *English Public Finance 1558–1641*, London, 1964
Haynes, Samuel and Murdin, William. eds., *A Collection of State Papers left by William Cecil*, Lord Burghley, London, 1740–59
Hillier, Caroline, *Bulwark Shore: Thanet and the Cinque Ports*, London, 1980
Hull, Felix, ed., *A Calendar of the White and Black Books of the Cinque Ports 1432–1955*, London, 1966
Neale, John, *Elizabeth I and her Parliaments*, London, 1950
Calendar of State Papers, Domestic, 1547–1603; Addenda, 1566–1579
Read, Conyers, *Mr Secretary Cecil and Queen Elizabeth*, London, 1955
Rowse, A.L., *The England of Elizabeth*, London, 1950
Simpson, W.S., *Chapters in the History of Old St Paul's*, London, 1881
Stow, John, *A Survey of London*, Oxford, 1908

5. Saving Virginia

Brown, Alexander, *The Genesis of the United States*, docs CCXVIII, CCXX-CCXXII, CCCXLII, CCCXLII, CCCXLVIII, Boston, 1891

Clode, Charles, *Memorials of the Merchant Taylors*, London, 1874

Craven, Wesley, *Dissolution of the Virginia Company*, New York, 1932

Kingsbury, Susan Myra, ed., *The Records of the Virginia Company of London*, Washington, 1906

Milton, Giles, *Big Chief Elizabeth*, London, 2000

Taylor, Alan, *American Colonies*, London, 2002

Three Proclamations Concerning the Lottery for 1613–1621, Providence, Rhode Island, 1907

Walne, Peter, 'The Running Lottery of the Virginia Company', *Virginia Magazine of History and Biography*, vol. 70 (1962), pp 30–34

6. Freeing the British Slaves of Barbary

Abulafia David, ed., *The Mediterranean in History*, London, 2003

Calendar of State Papers, Addenda, 1660–1670

Colley, Linda, *Captives*, London, 2002

Earle, Peter, *Corsairs of Malta and Barbary*, London, 1970

Fisher, Godfrey, *Barbary Legend: War, Trade and Piracy in North Africa 1415–1830*, Oxford, 1957

Mercurius Publicus

The Journals of Sir Thomas Allin 1660–78, ed. Roger Anderson, London 1939–40

7. Cashing in on Speculative Fever – Thomas Neale

Anon, An *Elegaick Essay upon the Decease of the Groom Porter and the Lotteries*, London, 1700

Anon, *Angliae Tutamen. The safety of England*, London, 1695

Anon, *Diluvium Lachrymarum. A review of the fortunate and unfortunate adventurers*, London, 1694

Evelyn, John, *Diary and Correspondence*, ed. William Bray, London 1906

Macaulay, Thomas, *The History of England from the accession of James II,* London, 1848–1861

Murphy, Anne, *Financial History Review*, No. 12, 10/9/2005

Neale, Thomas, *A Profitable Adventure for the Fortunate and can be unfortunate to none*, London, 1693

Neale, Thomas, The *Prizes Drawn at the Profitable Adventure to the Fortunate in Freeman's Yard at Cornhill*, London, 1693

Picard, Lisa, *Restoration London*, London, 1997

8. Cashing in on Speculative Fever – John Blunt

Balen, Malcolm, *A Very English Deceit: The Secret History of the South Sea Bubble and the First Great Financial Scandal*, London, 2002

Chancellor, Edward, *Devil Take the Hindmost: A History of Financial Speculation*, Basingstoke, 1999

Post Boy 17–20/02/1711
Post Boy 10/03/1711
Post Boy 15/03/1711
Post Boy 5–8/05/1711
The Daily Courant 13/03/1711
The Examiner 8–15/03/1711

9. Lover of Money – Casanova

Casanova, Giacomo, *History of My Life*, Longmans, London, 1968
Dunkley, John, *Gambling: a social and moral problem in France, 1685–1792*, Oxford, 1985
Masters, John, *Casanova*, London, 2001
Stigler, Stephen, *Casanova's Lottery*, University of Chicago Record, Vol. 37, No. 10, 12/06/2003

10. Fleecing the Public – Charles 'Patch' Price

Roberts, Richard and Kynaston, David, eds., *The Bank of England: Money, Power and Influence 1694–1699*, Oxford, 1995
Tomalin, Claire, *Samuel Pepys*, London, 2002
William Hone's Everyday Book, 1826
Wilkinson, George, *The Newgate Calendar* 1–3, London, 1962

11. Founding the British Museum – Swindler Peter Leheup

Caygill, Marjorie, *The Story of the British Museum*, London, 2002
Cobbett, William, *Parliamentary History of England 1066–1803*, vol. XV, London, 1813
Edwards, Edward, *Lives of the Founders, and Notices of some Chief Benefactors and Organisers of the British Museum*, London 1870
Miller, Edward, *That Noble Cabinet, A History of the British Museum*, London, 1973
Report from the Committee appointed to examine the Book containing an Account of the Contributors to the Lottery 1753, House of Commons, 1754
Wilson, David, *The British Museum: a history*, London, 2002

12. Lottery Mania – Late Eighteenth Century

Foreman, Amanda, *Georgiana, Duchess of Devonshire*, London, 1998
Hicks, Carola, *Improper Pursuits: the Scandalous Life of Lady Di Beauclerk*, London, 2001
Lloyd's Evening Post and *British Chronicle* 23/11/1767
Raven, James, 'The Abolition of the English State Lotteries', *The Historical Journal*, vol. 34 (1991), pp 371–389

The Autobiography of Francis Place 1771–1854, ed. Mary Thrale, Cambridge, 1972
The Gazetteer and *New Daily Advertiser* 20/11/1767
The London Evening Post 28/11/1767
The Public Advertiser 20/11/1767

13. Arch Opponent – William Wilberforce

Buxton, Thomas, *An Inquiry Whether Crime and Misery are Produced or Prevented by our Present System of Prison Discipline*, London, 1813
Cowie, Leonard, *William Wilberforce 1759–1833, A Bibliography*, London, 1992
Parliamentary Select Committee Reports on laws relating to lotteries; First Report (pp147–50) 13/04/1808, Second Report (pp 151–237), 24/06/1808
The Correspondence of William Wilberforce, London, 1840
Wilberforce, Robert, Isaac and Samuel, *The Life of William Wilberforce*, London, 1838

14. Pioneer of Advertising – Thomas Bish

Bish, Thomas, *A collection of handbills and newspaper cuttings relating to lotteries, chiefly issued by T. Bish*, British Library Collection
Bish, Thomas, *A collection of miscellaneous items re lotteries 1726–1826*, 2 vols, Guildhall Library
Hansard, *Parliamentary History of England*, vols XIV–XVII, 1826–1827; vols IX–XXXIX, 1832–1837
Nevett, Terry, *Advertising in Britain: A History*, London, 1982

15. Mystical View – Charles Lamb

Burton, Sarah, *A Double Life: A Biography of Charles and Mary Lamb*, London, 2003
Courtenay, Winifred, *Young Charles Lamb 1775–1802*, London, 1982
Lucas, Edward, ed., *The Works of Charles and Mary Lamb*, London, 1903–1905
Strachan, John, 'Man is a Gaming Animal. Lamb, Gambling and Thomas Bish's Last Lottery', *The Charles Lamb Bulletin*, No. 109, 2000

16. Never Told a Lie? – George Washington

Ellis, Joseph, *His Excellency: George Washington*, London, 2004
Flexner, James, *George Washington*, Boston, 1965–1972
Freeman, Douglas, *George Washington: a biography*, London, 1948–1957
McMaster, John, *The History of the People of the United States, from the Revolution to the Civil War*, New York, 1883–1913
The Papers of George Washington, eds. William Abbot and Dorothy Twohig, Charlottesville, 1992
Tindall, William, *Standard History of the City of Washington*, Knoxville, 1914

17. Louisiana State Lottery – Most Corrupt Ever

Brooks, Henry, *Curiosities of the Old Lottery: Gleanings Chiefly from the Old Newspapers of Boston and Salem*, Boston, 1866
Ezell, John, *Fortune's Merry Wheel: the Lottery in America*, Cambridge, Mass, 1960
Kendall, John, *History of New Orleans*, Chicago, 1922
Ralph, Julian, *Dixie*, New York, 1896
Tyson, Job, *Brief Survey of the Great Extent and Evil Tendencies of the Lottery System as Existing in the United States*, Philadelphia, 1833

18. It Never Could Be You

Douglas, Andrew, *The National Lottery and its Regulation*, London, 2001
Financial Mail on Sunday, 3/6/2007
Financial Times, 4/10/2002
Keynes, John Maynard, *A Treatise on Probability*, London, 1921
Snoddy, Raymond and Ashworth, Jon, *It Could Be You. The Untold Story of the UK National Lottery*, London, 2000
The Guardian Weekend, 6/11/2004
The National Lottery Dream Study, Camelot, 2007
The National Lottery Millionaire Survey, MORI, 2006
The Observer, 3/11/2002
The Observer, 15/8/2004
The Sun, 11/8/2004

19. Does the Future Belong to Big Brother?

Addison, Tony and Chowdhury, Abdur, *A Global Lottery and a Global Premium Bond*, United Nations University, 2003
The Guardian Media, 12/8/2002
The Observer, 22/5/2005

20. Crackpots or Visionaries?

Barnett, Anthony and Carty, Peter, *The Athenian Option: radical reform for the House of Lords*, Demos, London, 1998
Carter, Francis, *Dubrovnik (Ragusa) – a classic city-state*, London, 1972
Davis, James, *Utopia and the ideal society: A study of English utopian writing 1516–1700*, Cambridge, 1981
Duxbury, Neil, *Random Justice*, Oxford, 1999
Evening Standard, 11/5/2007
Firth, Charles, ed., *Memoirs of Edmund Ludlow*, Oxford, 1894
Gardiner, Samuel, *History of the Commonwealth and Protectorate*, London, 1903
Goodwin, Barbara, *Justice by Lottery*, Hemel Hempstead, 1992
Googh, George, *History of English Democratic Ideas in the Seventeenth Century*, Cambridge, 1898

Streater, John, *Government Described, with a brief model of the Free-State of Ragouse*, London, 1659
The Mail on Sunday, 17/6/2007
The Observer, 21/10/2006
The Observer, 13/05/2007
The Sutton Trust, *Ballots in School Admissions,* 2007
Washington Post, 25/05/1985

Rollover 1: Scams Ancient and Modern

Anon, *Seasonable Words of Advice to all such as are concerned in the Lottery,* 1780
Anon, *Calculations and Facts relative to Lottery Insurances,* London, 1795
Colquhoun, Patrick, *A Treatise on the Police of the Metropolis,* 1796
Francis, John, *Chronicles and Characters of the Stock Exchange,* London, 1855
King, Richard, *The Frauds of London Detected,* London, 1780
The Wai Seng Lottery, *Straits Branch of the Royal Asiatic Society,* Singapore, 1895
Waller, Maureen, *1700: Scenes from London Life,* London, 2000
www.oldbaileyonline.org
House of Commons Culture, Media and Sport Committee Report on Call TV quiz shows, 17.1.2007
Private Eye, August 2005, quoting Kansas City Star, 12.05.2005
The Daily Telegraph, 31.01.2004
The Guardian, 26.02.2007

Rollover 2: From Fielding to Dalziel and Pascoe

Lamford, Paul, *Lottery Laughter, an anthology of lottery cartoons,* Cartoon Arts Trust, London, 1999
Rhinehart Luke, *The Dice Man,* London, 1972
Schama, Simon, The *embarrassment of riches. An interpretation of Dutch culture in the Golden Age,* London, 1987
Uglow, Jennifer, *William Hogarth: a life and a world,* London, 1997

ACKNOWLEDGEMENTS

Thank you to the staff of the British Library, particularly the Rare Books Room, Cambridge University Library, Cambridgeshire Library Service, the Guildhall Library and the National Archives at Kew. All were patient and efficient.

To Camelot and the National Lottery Commission for their prompt response to enquiries, Janet Huskinson for checking the Roman and Greek chapters, and my wife Carola for her sharp comments on the text. Any mistakes are mine alone.

The Virginia Company's splendid and unique lottery broadside is reproduced by kind permission of the Society of Antiquaries of London. The witty cartoons that light up the narrative were the product of the fertile mind of my old colleague, Simon Groves.

Finally, a big thank you to The History Press for giving me the opportunity to explore forgotten episodes in the quirky history of the lottery, which so often reflects the irrationality and unpredictability of life itself.

INDEX